The Richest of Fare

. . . .

To Pat,
Enjoy the feast,
Phyllis Strupp

The Richest of Fare

· · · · · · · · · · · · · · · · · · ·

Seeking Spiritual Security in the Sonoran Desert

Phyllis Strupp

Come, all you who are thirsty,
come to the waters;
and you who have no money,
come, buy and eat!
Come, buy wine and milk
without money and without cost.
Why spend your money on what is not bread,
and your labor on what does not satisfy?
Listen, listen to me, and eat what is good,
and your soul will delight in the richest of fare.

ISAIAH 55:1–2

SONORAN CROSS PRESS

SCOTTSDALE, ARIZONA

The photographs on the pages listed are the work of the following photographers and are reproduced with kind permission:

Margery N. Jenkins   96–97
Glenn B. Jenks   4, 16, 27, 45, 46, 50, 64, 68, 74, 98, 132, 146, 166, 195, 225
Douglas Stavoe   77, 107, 116, 202
Suzann Wilson   v, 21, 103, 207
Corel Stock Photography   120
All other photographs are the author's.

Sonoran Cross Press LLC
8912 East Pinnacle Peak Road, Suite 604
Scottsdale, Arizona 85255
www.desertspirituality.com

ISBN 0-9746727-0-X

*Library of Congress
Control Number
2003098440*

Design and composition by Barbara Jellow. Text is set in Scala, display in Perpetua Italic and Fine Hand. Paper stock is Gold East. Produced by Princeton Editorial Associates, Inc., Scottsdale, Arizona, www.princetoneditorial.com.
Printing and binding through Asia Pacific Offset.
Printed in Hong Kong.

9 8 7 6 5 4 3 2 1

Frontispiece: Heavy winter rains bring a nourishing flow of water through a wash in the Saguaro National Monument east of Tucson, Arizona.

Opposite: Lone Mountain witnesses yet another glorious sunset in the upper Sonoran Desert.

For Peter

· · · · ·

CONTENTS

Opposite: A view toward the south from Font's Point near Borrego Springs overlooks the Borrego badlands in California's Sonoran Desert.

PREFACE

*T*his book will help you to paint the "you are here" dot on the map of your spiritual life.

Based on the events of daily life, it is reasonable to wonder what kind of universe we live in. Albert Einstein once said that the most important question one can ask is this: Is the universe a friendly place?

Clearly Einstein believed there could be more than one response. Yet in today's world it is difficult to imagine answering "yes."

Although he died in 1955, Einstein was quite familiar with the problems that continue to plague our world today, including war, terrorism, weapons of mass destruction, religious intolerance, and institutional corruption. Yet he asked this question.

Today we know more than we ever have about the various risks and threats that the physical world presents. The universe can be a friendly place only in the spiritual sense, rather than the physical. And Einstein knew this. *His was a trick question.*

How can we find our way to a friendly universe, and experience the calmness and joy of spiritual security?

Fortunately, in today's world, achievement of spiritual security is easier than ever before. We have at hand all the tools we need to paint the "you are here" dot on the map of our spiritual lives:

Direct experience with Nature, gained through our senses.

Intellectual knowledge about the world, gained through science.

Intuitive understanding of life, gained through our spiritual traditions.

So many of us are unaware of the difference between religion and spirituality. Religion is a human creation, and as such it often tends to divide people. Spirituality is a divine gift to humanity, and as such it is based on universal values that connect all of us with our own selves, each other, Nature, and God.

These timeless spiritual values are the richest of fare for the human soul, leading it to spiritual security and steering it away from violence and death. Religion is the servant of spirituality, not the other way around.

In seeking a friendly universe and spiritual security, there is no need to recreate the wheel. For several thousand years, humanity has been struggling with the very same threats that we face today. Only the weapons have changed.

Just as civilization has produced such intellectual geniuses as Charles Darwin and Albert Einstein, it has also yielded spiritual geniuses who have left behind valuable insights about universal spiritual values and the way home. Their teachings have been validated, not nullified, as we accumulate scientific findings about the nature of the universe.

The Desert has played a crucial role in the lives of many of these spiritual geniuses: Abraham. Moses. David. Isaiah. John the Baptist. Jesus. Mohammed.

Walk with me through these pages as we explore how to use the tools of the Sonoran Desert's nature, our current understanding of the world, and the Bible in our quest for spiritual security.

Each chapter of this book follows a similar pattern. Four quotes set the stage— one each from the Old Testament, the New Testament gospels and epistles, and literature. Stories about Desert life lead to larger issues, which are considered from both current and biblical perspectives. Color pictures from the Sonoran Desert and quotes are interspersed throughout the text to highlight important themes. Personal reflections appear in italics.

Like yours, no doubt, my personal spiritual journey has taken many twists and turns. Mine has included a Roman Catholic upbringing and twenty years outside organized religion. For the past ten years, I have been part of the Episcopalian faith community.

This book shares some of the ground I have covered to place my own "you are here" dot. My hope is that it will help you in your own search for spiritual security.

Carefree, Arizona
October 20, 2003

. . . . .

Thus says the Lord:
Stand at the crossroads, and look,
and ask for the ancient paths
where the good way lies;
and walk in it,
and find rest for your souls.
JEREMIAH 6:16

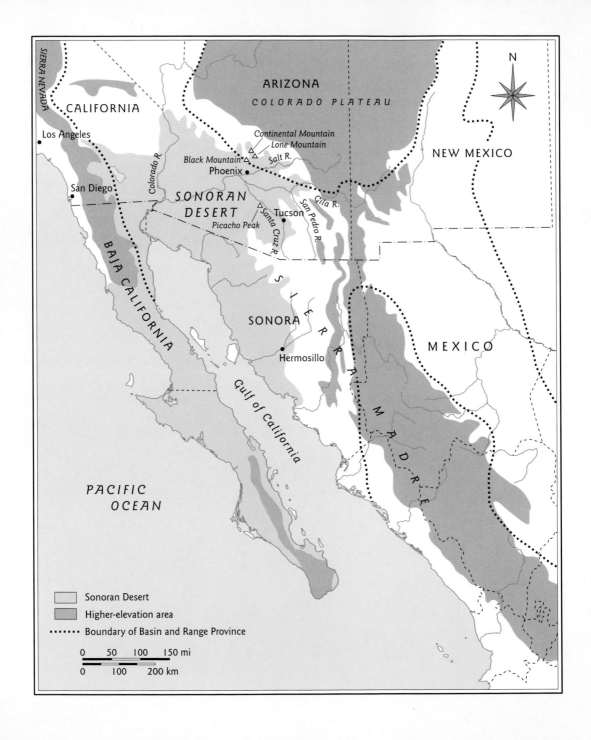

The Richest of Fare

· · · · · · · · · · · · · · · · ·

Prologue

In returning and rest you shall be saved;
in quietness and in trust shall be your strength.
GOD, ISAIAH 30:15 NRSV

Come with me by yourselves to a quiet place and get some rest.
JESUS TO HIS DISCIPLES, MARK 6:31

For everything that was written in the past was written to teach us, so that through
endurance and the encouragement of the Scriptures we might have hope.
PAUL, ROMANS 15:4

The first going-down into the desert is always something of a surprise.
Where and how did we gain the idea that the desert was merely a sea of sand?
JOHN C. VAN DYKE, *The Desert*

Opposite: Blue sky, sun, mountains, and the
saguaro cactus define the Sonoran Desert's character.

*T*here's something about land.

That mixture of soil, rocks, landforms, air, light, water, plants, animals, sights, sounds, textures, scents, flavors: the land, the place where we live. Always there, in so many ways, supporting us, nourishing us, restoring us. Our home, our refuge, the very ground of our being: the land.

Land is useful to us in so many ways.

But what do you do with a land like this—this land called the Sonoran Desert?

A tortured land, born of volcanic violence over the past thirty million years.

A rugged land, sculpted by raging floods and pounding winds over the past five million years.

An arid land, withered by too much sun and too little rain for ten thousand years.

A bizarre land, inhabited by a unique collection of plants and animals for four thousand years.

A forsaken land, haunted by the remains of a civilization that mysteriously vanished seven hundred years ago.

A fragile land, threatened by habitat destruction and declining biodiversity over the past forty years.

What do you do with a land like this—this land called the Sonoran Desert?

The best and highest use of this scraggly land is not readily apparent.

Blade it, grade it, build it out, some say. That is its best and highest use.

Yet amid the dust and devastation, another voice is being heard on the best and highest use of this land.

Preserve it, so we can walk, hike, and ride in the Desert.

Preserve it, so we can watch, listen, and wonder in the Desert.

Preserve it, so we can read, learn, and pray in the Desert.

Preserve it, so we might truly be alive in the Desert.

Preserve it, so future generations might learn the Desert's secrets.

Here life's rhythm is a slave to the oppressive sun, the fickle rains, and the punishing winds. These harsh elements give the Desert a rough edge that exfoliates all who enter, preparing them for renewal.

Various conquerors and refugees have invaded this area repeatedly over the past two thousand years, each on a personal quest for the good life while cutting a path of destruction through the Desert's tender hide. Most sojourners have left unfulfilled, blindly passing by the Desert's richest offerings.

In the 1500s, Spanish explorers first entered the current Mexican state of Sonora, for which the Sonoran Desert is named. They discovered impressive deposits of iron ore, which at that time was used primarily for making bells. So they named the region Sonora, Spanish for "sonorous."

Centuries later, the Sonoran Desert is living up to her name. She is one huge bell measuring 120,000 square miles across Arizona, California, and Mexico. And she is ringing loud and clear, trying to give us a wake-up call before it's too late.

The Desert is trying to wake us up to the spiritual truth about our existence. Spiritual security is close at hand and freely available to all, even in today's world haunted by consumption, corruption, fanaticism, weapons of mass destruction, and environmental devastation.

For thousands of years, spiritual geniuses such as Abraham, Moses, David, Isaiah, John the Baptist, Jesus, and Mohammed have found that the path to spiritual security led right into the Desert. They were on to something—and it's time we followed their lead.

This wild, prickly place is ready to do what she was created to do.

The Desert is ready to help us find our place in the universe.

The Desert is ready to help us rediscover our spiritual traditions, born as they were in the Desert.

The Desert is ready to help us understand the universal spiritual truths that bring meaning to life.

After almost three thousand years, the voice of one calling in the desert has become the voice of the Desert herself.

Let's see what she has to say.

· · · · ·

ONE

Cosmos

And when you look up to the sky and see the sun, the moon and the stars—all the heavenly array—do not be enticed into bowing down to them and worshipping.
MOSES, DEUTERONOMY 4:19

There will be signs in the sun, moon and stars. . . . Men will faint from terror, apprehensive of what is coming on the world, for the heavenly bodies will be shaken.
JESUS, LUKE 21:25–26

For since the creation of the world God's invisible qualities— his eternal power and divine nature—have been clearly seen, being understood from what has been made, so that men are without excuse.
PAUL, ROMANS 1:20

Consider frequently the connection of all things in the universe and their relation to one another. For things are somehow implicated with one another, and all in a way friendly to one another.
MARCUS AURELIUS, *Meditations*

Opposite: The moon near daybreak above the Four Peaks wilderness area.

*W*herever you are, you know what's up.

So vast, so there, so everywhere, it is taken for granted: the sky.

Here in the northern reaches of the Sonoran Desert where we live, if you happen to look up during the day, chances are that a bright sun in a sea of blue will greet you.

If you happen to look up at night, chances are that dark skies and a starry host will greet you. After the sun has relinquished his rule, a host of twinkling stars appears, led by the moon and the planets when their orbits allow. Away from the urban glow, the Desert often provides dry, clear night skies, revealing many of the six thousand or so stars that are visible to the naked eye.

Gazing at this reassuring spectacle of night lights, the origin of the word *disaster* (from the Latin for "away" and "star") seems quite sensible. For the Romans, to be apart from the stars was to lose one's way—literally, since they relied on celestial navigation.

Around here, many people continue to feel as the Romans did about seeing the stars at night. The term *dark skies* is a battle cry for those fighting the advance of towering, harsh lighting on the suburban and rural fringes of the cities.

Only clouds stood between the stars and the Romans. Now murky politics and zoning gymnastics put blinding lights between stars and people.

A real disaster.

One could reasonably ask why sentiments regarding dark skies run so strong around here. Is there anything much to see?

Pondering the night sky appears to be a peculiarly human inclination, and one that has contributed much to the development of civilization. Observation of celestial bodies spurred the development of agriculture, religion, and science many thousands of years ago.

The orderly habits of the sun, moon, planets, and stars spoke of order to our ancestors. Indeed, long ago they organized our calendar of twenty-four-hour days, seven-day weeks, thirty-day-or-so months, and twelve-month years according to these habits.

But that was then, and this is now.

We don't navigate by the stars as the Romans did. Most of us are not farmers. Besides, we have better things to do than people of long ago.

Or do we?

Have we forgotten something they knew? Maybe we should look up and see what is there.

Perhaps we could use more order in our lives.

It would be well, perhaps, if we were to spend more of our days and	Dark skies
nights without any obstruction between us and the celestial bodies.	. . . . .
HENRY DAVID THOREAU, *Walden*	

Dark skies take some getting used to, but they have a lot to offer to those who take the time to become acquainted with their ways. As a beginner, it is easy to be deceived by airplane lights and satellites, but soon enough these imposters can be seen for what they are.

Night and day are the defining events of life on Earth. Nevertheless, sunset and dawn occur within subtle transitions lasting up to ninety minutes—giving everyone on Earth plenty of time to prepare for what's coming.

At the end of the day, when the sun begins decorating the mountains with a rosy honey glow, the show begins.

As the Earth continues to turn away from the sun, he refuses to let her go. His long infrared rays linger to caress the Earth's atmosphere with a blushing embrace, visible in the eastern sky especially in the winter months, when the Earth and sun are farthest apart.

As the sun and the Earth slowly let go of each other, the Earth's dark, blue-gray shadow appears briefly on the eastern horizon before vanishing into the night. Yes, the Earth has a shadow, just as everyone else does; her substantial presence casts an impressive silhouette against the evening sky.

The first night lights to appear are not usually the stars, but the moon and the planets, depending on their orbits. They become visible quickly in the twilight, since they shine not by emitting their own light but by reflecting sunlight.

Long before the sun sets the moon might be out, depending on where she is in her travels. Or she might rise after the planets and even the stars have become visible. When she's full or close to it, she ascends in the night sky with an anguished expression. Later in the evening, as she descends from the top of the sky, her grimace turns into a smirk.

> *We praise You, Lord, for*
> *Sister Moon and the Stars,*
> *in the heavens you have made*
> *them bright, precious and fair.*
> FRANCIS OF ASSISI,
> *"The Canticle of Brother Sun"*

That playful Sister Moon.

While the planets may have orderly paths, their appearances are quite eccentric. Around Christmas one year, Venus put on a lengthy evening "Star of Bethlehem" display in the western sky for weeks; the next year, she was nowhere to be seen. The following December, she dominated the eastern sky as the morning star.

Similarly, Mercury, Mars, Jupiter, and Saturn might really show off or not even show up at certain times of the year, all according to the tyrannical demands of their orbits.

Gradually and gracefully, the stars join the party. They appear only when the sky is very dark, since they are so far away from our solar system and shine from their own internally generated light.

Flickering stars may display hues of green, blue, red, orange, or yellow produced by various burning gases.

These fiery giants appear so gentle and peaceful from our vantage point millions of miles away. Yet some of the largest stars are so big that our entire solar system could fit into one of them.

Every now and then, a shooting star whizzes by, as if God has just winked at you.

On most nights some of the Earth's inhabitants can see a creamy, radiant path of stars spreading from northeast to southwest, revealing the prominent feature for which our galaxy is named: the Milky Way. About two-thirds of the world's people cannot see the Milky Way on any given night because of the interference of artificial light.

Even without the menace of artificial light, most constellations are hard to spot because they bear no resemblance to their names. However, the Big Dipper is a welcome exception, and is easily seen.

Looking to the north from our driveway, sometimes the Big Dipper starts the night with its handle buried in the top of nearby Continental Mountain, as if the mountain is wielding the dipper to avenge its defacement at the hands of man and machines. At other times, the Big Dipper hangs directly overhead, apparently full of nothing but darkness.

The North Star, which is always aligned with the axis of the Earth, can easily be found off the front of the Big Dipper's cup. Because the North Star's position in the sky doesn't change, it has for centuries been especially useful in navigation.

The North Star always shows the way home here on Earth.

The stars are the apexes of what wonderful triangles! What distant and different beings in the various mansions of the universe are contemplating the same one at the same moment!

HENRY DAVID THOREAU, *Walden*

The Little Dipper is also easy to find, since its stars are clustered closely together and it looks like a dipper. Sometimes it faces the Big Dipper, as if to scoop up what flows out from the greater source.

Orion, the celestial hunter, is easily located because of the two perpendicular rows of stars that form his belt and sword. This constellation includes one of the brightest stars in the night sky: Betelgeuse.

While many civilizations from around the world have woven tales of adventure about this mighty hunter, around here he often kicks back. Orion might start the evening napping to the east of us on nearby Lone Mountain, before he lunges up to challenge the night with his dazzling bow and arrow.

As the night slips away, the Earth slowly turns back toward the sun. Then the drama of sunrise, a perfect reversal of sunset, unfolds softly in the sky and on the land.

Just Another Day

The light which puts out our eyes is darkness to us.
HENRY DAVID THOREAU, *Walden*

. . . . .

As dawn approaches, the long red rays of the sun gently awaken the atmosphere and the mountains in the west with a warm hug. The Earth's shadow appears, and then gradually the sky lightens to the bright blue color we see.

The sky is not actually blue: we just see it that way. While sunshine includes the entire color spectrum, air molecules scatter more of the shorter, ultraviolet light rays than other rays, so we generally see a blue sky. The longer infrared rays are visible only at sunrise and sunset.

Before we know it, the sun is up and a new day has arrived.

Just another day. Thank God for just another day here on Earth.

All day long, the moon, planets, and stars are still up there in the sky watching over us, but they're rendered invisible by the sun's brightness. Beyond the atmosphere, the dark night sky is the constant background of the universe, and the sun appears as just another star in the sky. There is no night and no day out there in space. Just ask any astronaut.

The Earth brings us day by turning toward the sun, and lets night return as she turns away from the sun. Faithfully, our night lights reappear to guide us through the darkness and remind us of how vast the universe is.

And to get us thinking.

Millions of years before human hands first crafted a dipper, the Big and Little Dippers were up in the sky, forming patterns that no one could appreciate. Of all things, why would there be two easily observed, different-sized dippers in the sky? Can that be a coincidence?

What are the Dippers trying to tell us?

When humans first looked up at the dark skies thousands of years ago, what were they thinking as they pondered the sparkling grandeur spread out above them?

Opposite: The sun's infrared rays and the Earth's shadow are visible in the western atmosphere at daybreak.

And not by eastern windows only,

When daylight comes, comes in the light,

In front, the sun climbs slow, how slowly,

But westward, look, the land is bright.

ARTHUR HUGH CLOUGH,
"Say Not the Struggle Naught Availeth"

Twinkle, twinkle, little star, how I wonder what you are.

Did the night sky's contrasts stimulate early human consciousness the way a black-and-white mobile stimulates a newborn's mind?

When humans first discovered that the celestial bodies move in predictable ways, was the newly found knowledge used to benefit everyone, or just a few?

Our ancestors understood that stargazing leads to questions. What is the universe? How did the universe come to be as it is—and what lies ahead for it? Why is there a universe—and why are we here? Is the universe a friendly place?

Questions that we all must ask for ourselves before we can ever find any answers.

Our Bipolar Universe

The universe is either a confusion, an intermingling of atoms, or it is unity and order and providence. If it is the former, why do I wish to tarry amid such a haphazard confusion and disorder?
MARCUS AURELIUS, *Meditations*

About twenty-five hundred years ago, the ancient Greeks coined the term *cosmos,* meaning all existing things regarded as an orderly, harmonious whole. The term *universe,* meaning all existing things, derives from the Latin for "turned into one."

Since the time when the ancient Greeks first pondered the cosmos, one of the greatest advances ever in understanding how it works resulted from Albert Einstein's revolutionary theories. Early in the twentieth century, Einstein's findings on relativity contradicted many commonly held scientific beliefs about the universe.

Einstein revealed a universe in which almost everything is relative—defined by its relationships. Time, location, matter, and motion are all relative, depending on the frame of reference (the observer's location and motion in space). The physical laws of Nature are the same for all observers in a given frame of reference.

Only the speed of light (186,000 miles per second) is constant throughout the universe, regardless of the speed of the light source or the observer. The speed of light determines the cosmic speed limit—nothing can travel faster than the speed of light.

Is there a spiritual equivalent to the speed of light?

These remarkable findings triggered an enormous paradigm shift within the scientific community about how the universe works. Over the past century, Einstein's work has facilitated many innovations, including nuclear power and weapons.

In terms of applying modern scientific findings about the universe to daily life, the most important thing to understand is that the universe has a bipolar disorder. Deeply imbedded within the universe's behavior are two conflicting traits: a tendency toward self-destruction and a tendency toward collaboration.

A cosmic self-destructive streak is apparent in the universe's rapidly accelerating expansion. From the beginning, the universe was inclined toward pushing outward from the center. However, at some point this inclination became an obsession, one that may eventually lead to its demise.

A mysterious substance called dark energy seems to be fueling the universe's expansion. This strange stuff does not emit radiation or light and has never been observed. However, it dominates the universe, accounting for three-fourths of the universe's mass, and it urges matter to push apart rather than pull together.

Dark energy acts like a cancerous tumor, delighting in suicidal, uncontrolled growth.

If it weren't for gravity, the universe might have come apart at the seams long ago. Even so, at this point in cosmic history dark energy seems to be gaining the

Nature has no one distinguishable ultimate tendency with which it is possible to feel a sympathy. In the vast rhythm of her processes, as the scientific mind now follows them, she appears to cancel herself out.

WILLIAM JAMES,
The Varieties of Religious Experience

upper hand against the attractive force of gravity, thereby accelerating the pace of the universe's expansion.

A self-destructive tendency is also evident in the universe's penchant for collisions. Energy, forces, particles, and matter are continually colliding during the course of daily life in the universe. Even though we cannot see most of these collisions with the naked eye, they appear to be the driving force behind most, if not all, observable phenomena. Colliding matter makes the universe go round—as when a sperm collides with an egg.

A collision occurs when somethingness runs into otherness.

The universe's inclination toward self-destruction is also evident from the make-up of ordinary matter. Its name notwithstanding, there is nothing ordinary about ordinary matter. It is a minority on the cosmic scene, accounting for only a sliver of the universe's mass (about 4 percent). In addition, ordinary matter has an unstable nature, since over 90 percent of its atoms are highly volatile hydrogen atoms and most of the remaining atoms are made of another volatile element, helium.

Self-destructive dark energy and hydrogen are the rulers of this world.

If it weren't for a tiny dose of heavier elements, such as oxygen, iron, and silica, that stabilize hydrogen, there would be no stars, galaxies, planets, rocks, water, plants, animals, people, buildings, cars, or money. There would be just explosive gases like hydrogen and helium.

Despite these self-destructive tendencies, somehow the universe also has a strong appetite for collaboration.

Would the universe have a collaborative streak if there were no dark energy or hydrogen?

We Are Stardust ․ ․ ․ ․ ․	*I hear you whispering there O stars of heaven. . . .* *If you do not say any thing how can I say any thing?* WALT WHITMAN, *"Song of Myself"*

Despite the pervasive presence of dark energy and hydrogen, the universe's collaborative streak has been strong enough to hold things together over the past fourteen billion years. The major cosmic collaborators are gravity, stars, and neutrinos.

Gravity is the only known force that affects everything in the universe. This is a relatively gentle, attractive force that causes objects to come together—whether they want to or not. The more massive an object is, the stronger its gravitational effect on other objects.

We know gravity personally—that's what keeps our feet on the ground so we don't float around like astronauts in space. Gravity sculpted cosmic debris into the sun, the Earth, and the moon. Gravity keeps the Earth revolving around the sun, and the moon revolving around the Earth.

Gravity brings order out of chaos.

In addition to gravity, the collaborative side of the universe's personality is evident in the behavior of stars and neutrinos (meaning "little neutral ones").

A few million years after the universe was born in an event known as the Big Bang, the first stars formed as heavier elements collided into each other and hung together thanks to gravity. These great glowing furnaces were fueled by the energy released as hydrogen and helium atoms fused together. Stars proliferated and clumped together in galaxies.

Since that time, stars have been evolving through a life cycle quite similar to our own: birth, growth, decline, and death.

Some stars, called black holes, implode when they die, caving in upon themselves and becoming incredibly dense—as if the sun had been squeezed into a golf ball. These stars become so small that they are invisible, yet each has a gravitational field so intense that nothing can escape from it—not even light.

Disappearing into the darkness of self-absorption—sounds like hell.

Other stars, called supernovas, do the opposite. They burn very brightly and then die through a spectacular explosion. Supernovas are the ultimate cosmic collaborators, birthing new life as they die.

Indeed, supernovas were responsible for dispersing the cosmic sliver of ordinary matter far and wide. As the universe aged, bursting supernovas scattered heavier elements such as carbon, iron, magnesium, nitrogen, oxygen, potassium,

and many others over vast distances. These elements were essential to the development of other celestial bodies, such as planets and moons, as well as life on Earth.

Everything we see is stardust—including us.

A supernova explosion seems to be triggered by the presence of neutrinos, elusive particles that do not seem to play much of a role in Nature. A neutrino is not part of an atom, has no electrical charge, and rarely interacts with other particles. Yet the unassuming neutrino ignites supernovas—thereby creating everything that is.

Above: Like everything else that can be observed, this curve-billed thrasher and Teddybear cholla cactus are made of the remnants of exploded stars.

Neutrinos are in the world, but not of the world.

Stars generate vast numbers of neutrinos, which constantly travel through space and matter—and even through us! For example, the sun generates an enormous stream of neutrinos; trillions of neutrinos occupy our bodies at every second. Neutrinos can even penetrate dense substances such as lead or the Earth's crust.

However, neutrinos are difficult to understand. For unknown reasons, as neutrinos travel from the sun to Earth they sometimes morph from one type of neutrino to another—from an electron neutrino, say, to a muon neutrino, to a tau neutrino, and possibly to other types as well. In addition, it is still a mystery why some stars have enough neutrinos to trigger a supernova explosion while other stars don't.

Neutrinos convert probabilities into possibilities.

Despite its bipolar personality, our universe is exceptionally good at its job of making stars. Currently, there are over one hundred billion galaxies in the observable universe, each one encompassing vast numbers of stars. Our galaxy alone has several hundred billion stars. The nearest one is the sun, which is about 4.6 billion years old and 93 million miles away from the Earth.

The dark skies of the Desert are a window on the soul of the cosmos.

Ground zero

Our inventions are wont to be pretty toys, which distract our attention from serious things. They are but improved means to an unimproved end, an end which it was already but too easy to arrive at.

HENRY DAVID THOREAU, *Walden*

Over the past fourteen billion years, the universe's life story has unfolded as the forces of self-destruction and collaboration have produced the Big Bang, energy, matter, elements, stars, light, heat, the sun, the Earth, the moon, the ocean, the atmosphere, life—and us.

Although it is truly amazing that so much of this story is known, a comprehensive understanding of the universe still eludes the scientific community. Despite his best efforts over several decades, Einstein himself was unsuccessful in crafting a grand unified theory that would describe all observable phenomena and eliminate known inconsistencies among existing theories.

We really don't know exactly what is going on in the physical universe.

Today, the search for a unified theory continues. Superstring theory has emerged as the leading contender, proposing that all natural phenomena can be explained by the movements of tiny stringlike loops that exist simultaneously in multiple dimensions of space and time. For this theory to hold true, there would have to be several more coexisting dimensions than the four now recognized—height, width, length, and time. However, many questions are still unanswered.

What might be going on in those other dimensions?

Even without a unified theory, perhaps modern science's greatest contribution to civilization has already been made: it has proven that the human soul exists.

As scientific achievements have blossomed over the past five hundred years, Western civilization has become highly skeptical about anything that cannot be observed through the five senses or analyzed with scientific methods.

This pervasive skepticism has also influenced our belief in the human soul. Is there a soul, or not? How can we be sure if we can't observe it, measure it, or predict it? Where's the evidence? Where's the proof?

Now modern science has finally proved that the human soul exists—although perhaps not in the way one might expect.

Just as the knee, the shoulder, the heart, the appendix, the liver, or any other body part goes unnoticed until injury or disease brings pain, so it is with the soul. Combine the natural instincts and creativity of our species with the technological advances of the past one hundred years, and what do we get?

The tanks and mustard gas of World War I.

The gas chambers and ovens of the Holocaust.

The air raids and atomic bombs of World War II.

The fighter planes and strafing runs of Korea.

Opposite: A saguaro can continue to stand over the Desert even after it dies.

Was somebody asking to see the soul?
See, your own shape and countenance,
   persons, substances, beasts, the trees,
the running rivers, the rocks and sands.
All hold spiritual joys and afterwards
   loosen them;
How can the real body ever die
   and be buried?

WALT WHITMAN,
"Starting from Paumanok"

The napalm and Agent Orange of Vietnam.

The Scud batteries and armored vehicles of Desert Storm.

The exploding jets and collapsing skyscrapers of 9/11.

The attack helicopters and satellite-guided missiles of the wars in Afghanistan and Iraq.

The suicide bombings of today's world.

As with our colleges, so with a hundred "modern improvements": there is an illusion about them; there is not always a positive advance.
HENRY DAVID THOREAU, *Walden*

Civilization's scientific advances have brought us an improved means to the unimproved end of killing one another, which has produced an unprecedented soul-ache in the human heart. The victors and the vanquished come and go, but the weapons keep getting better and the soul-ache keeps getting worse.

Of course we have a soul—that's what hurts so bad.

A soul-ache so acute that no diversion or pleasure can distract from it.

A soul-ache so intense that no medication or addiction can ease it.

A soul-ache so painful that the soul's existence can no longer be denied.

A soul-ache so deep that our basic assumptions about life must be reconsidered.

Einstein said that the most important question to ask oneself is this: Is the universe a friendly place?

A friend is someone you know, like, and trust. Can we know, like, and trust the universe?

The universe revealed through science does not seem like a friendly place.

This is a forbidding, unknowable place that defies the limits of human comprehension.

This is an unpredictable place, where collisions, violence, decay, and death are parts of daily life.

This is a mysterious place where self-destructive dark energy seems to be overwhelming collaborative gravity.

Opposite: A solar eclipse appears over the Desert.

But for you who revere my name
the sun of righteousness shall rise,
with healing in its wings.

GOD, MALACHI 4:2 NRSV

Our universe does not seem like a friendly place—but it is trying to be.

The collaborative heart of the universe has not stopped beating yet. It wants our help in making the universe a place where Nature and humanity can live together without the threats of violence and self-destruction.

Dark energy is being transformed into a collaborative agent.

A place that offers a home where our souls can stop aching and find rest and peace.

A place that offers a home that everyone can afford, because humility is the only down payment required.

A place where everything and everyone has purpose and meaning.

This sounds like a friendly place—a place that we can know, like, and trust.

Despite the apparent hostility of our universe, over the centuries many people (including Einstein) have been able to see our universe as a friendly place. However, the first people to notice the universe's friendliness did not look through telescopes—they looked up at the dark skies of the Middle Eastern Desert.

spiritual Relativity
. . . . .

Listen. . . . I had another dream, and this time the sun and moon and eleven stars were bowing down to me.
JOSEPH, GENESIS 37:9

Almost three thousand years before Einstein introduced his theories concerning relativity in the physical universe, a small group of Hebrews living in the Middle East were the first to understand spiritual relativity: human beings are defined by their relationships.

These Hebrews were the first to forge a personal and even friendly relationship between the universe's higher power (God) and humanity. They came to believe that an almighty, omnipotent Creator made the universe and influenced the course of human affairs to accomplish the divine purpose.

God is up to something.

One of their names for God was "Yahweh" (meaning "I am who I am")—really a statement about God rather than a name. For them, the act of naming someone conveyed power over the one named—but Yahweh was beyond human comprehension and control, and thus couldn't be named. Even the word *Yahweh* was considered too holy to say, and so was spoken infrequently and reverently.

How did they know that Yahweh was real?

Like other ancient peoples, the Hebrews shared stories that explained how relationships between the divine, Nature, and people came to be as they found them. These stories were passed on orally for many generations, and eventually were incorporated into Genesis, the first book of the Hebrew scriptures (the Old Testament of the Bible).

Even today, many of these narratives are familiar, such as the stories of Adam and Eve, Noah's ark, and Cain and Abel, which we will explore in later chapters.

Undoubtedly, the thoughts expressed in the stories of Genesis were divinely inspired. However, such inspiration most often came through dreams, visions, or intuition rather than divine dictation. And so these stories are most valuable for their perspective on human relationships rather than for providing a historical account of the universe's evolution.

A common theme throughout the stories of Genesis is that a human being is defined by his or her relationships with God, Creation (Nature), other people, and self.

Human beings are spiritually defined by their relationships—just like the universe's physical matter.

The first chapter of Genesis explains how the Hebrews believed the world came to be as it is. From the void, God created everything in the universe in an orderly manner over the course of six days:

Day 1: Light, day, night

Day 2: Sky

Day 3: Dry land, seas, vegetation, seed-based reproduction

Day 4: Sun, moon, stars

Day 5: Marine life, birds, sexual reproduction

Day 6: Land animals, human beings

And on the seventh day, God rested.

This ancient version of how Creation unfolded over time is similar in several major ways to the current scientific theory of the universe's evolution. Darkness, light, and sky came first, then Earth and seas. Plants and marine animals came before land animals, and human beings came last.

God saw all that he had made, and it was very good. And there was evening, and there was morning—the sixth day. Thus the heavens and the earth were completed in all their vast array.

GENESIS 1:31–2:1

While darkness and light came first, the sun, the moon, and the stars were thought to have come after the Earth had been created, because clearly God created them to bring order to the Earth, as described in Genesis 1:14–15:

Let there be lights in the expanse of the sky to separate the day from the night, and let them serve as signs to mark seasons and days and years, and let them be lights in the expanse of the sky to give light on the earth.

Genesis portrays God as a thoughtful being who created with a purpose in mind, as well as an omnipotent being who created by speaking words. The divinely ordered knowledge, or the word of God, became the Creation.

To believe in God is to believe that everything and everyone in the Creation has a purpose.

God was pleased with every aspect and creature of the Creation, seeing that all was good. From the beginning, order, life, growth, and wholeness have been the divine will for the entire Creation.

The universe's collaborative streak is God's will.

Genesis lays out the ground rules for the relationships that spiritually define a human being—the relationships with God, Creation, others, and self.

Throughout the rest of the Old Testament, the Hebrews recorded the dimensions of their struggles to understand God's will and answer the question "Given Yahweh's will, how should we live?" Despite the teachings of Moses and the prophets, they had relationship difficulties with God amid the social, economic, and political challenges of daily life.

Even so, throughout the eighteen centuries covered by the Old Testament, the Hebrews preserved a deep yearning to do right by God and to remain in right relationship (righteous) with God. They passed this yearning for righteousness from generation to generation like a valuable treasure, nestled within the words of their oral tradition and holy scriptures.

However, no Hebrew yearned to be in right relationship with God more eloquently than David, who lived around three thousand years ago and authored many of the beautiful, heart-wrenching psalms.

By the word of the Lord were the heavens made,
their starry host by the breath of his mouth.
DAVID, PSALM 33:6

Listening
to the Stars
. . . . .

One of the earliest Hebrew kings, David was a beloved, charismatic ruler as well as an accomplished warrior. After his successful showdown with the giant Goliath, he quickly rose to power on the battlefield and in politics. During his thirty-year reign, which began around 1000 BC, he conquered a large portion of Palestine, giving the Hebrews the largest and most politically stable empire they were ever to have.

Although David's reign was like a Hebrew version of Camelot, his political and military triumphs did not endure. After the reign of his ambitious son Solomon ended in 924 BC, the empire broke apart into the two kingdoms of Israel and Judah. The Hebrews were troubled by political instability and foreign invasions for the next thousand years, until the Romans destroyed their temple in Jerusalem and expelled them from Palestine in AD 70.

David's more abiding legacy is the collection of psalms he wrote. In them he captured the highs and the lows of the human heart with compelling language, unlike anyone before or after him. These prayerful songs reveal a uniquely intimate, tender, yet reverent relationship with God. By turns they express praise, thanks, awe, respect, trust, hope, love, and faith, as well as fear, abandonment, confusion, ambition, hostility, anger, envy, shame, and remorse.

David understood what it means to have a soul-ache.

Throughout the psalms, David admired and proclaimed the manifold works of God in the Creation as he longed to be in right relationship with God. He believed the whole Creation depends on God for its survival. However, humanity depends on God not only for physical needs, but also for moral guidance and spiritual security.

The word of God—the spiritual equivalent of the speed of light.

Apparently, David was an inveterate stargazer. Several of his psalms mention the heavens and the stars, which he viewed as signs of God's concerned involvement in the cosmic order. Yet David did more than just gaze at the stars. He also listened to them with his heart, as Psalm 19:1–4 makes clear:

> The heavens declare the glory of God;
> the skies proclaim the work of his hands.
> Day after day they pour forth speech;
> night after night they display knowledge.
> There is no speech or language
> where their voice is not heard.
> Their voice goes out into all the earth,
> their words to the ends of the world.

That was David—slaying his enemies on the battlefield by day, playing music by night.

David saw the universe as a friendly place because of God's presence in it and concern for it. Despite the troubles, betrayals, and violence that haunted his life, he persistently yearned to be in right relationship with God.

On the battlefield of life, David's enduring victory deeply inspired many that came after him, including his most famous descendant—Jesus of Nazareth, born almost a thousand years later.

David charted the dimensions of the human heart, and Jesus showed us how to transcend them.

Opposite: A rare pool of water in the Desert offers welcome relief to many animals.

As a deer longs for flowing streams,
so my soul longs for you, O God.
My soul thirsts for God, for the living God.

When shall I come and behold
the face of God?

DAVID, PSALM 42:1–2 NRSV

*So in everything, do to others what you would have them do to you,
for this sums up the Law and the Prophets.*

JESUS, MATTHEW 7:12

Jesus was born into a devoutly religious family, descended from the House of David through both parents. Even as a youth, he spent time at the temple studying the Hebrew scriptures. These writings were probably similar to today's Old Testament and constituted Jesus' Bible, since the New Testament was written decades after his death.

At the age of thirty, Jesus left behind his family and career as an artisan and began a three-year public ministry of educating and healing. His teachings were deeply rooted in his Hebrew spiritual inheritance, especially the writings of Moses, David, and Isaiah.

Drawing on this rich heritage, Jesus had a unique gift for looking beyond the letter of the law and understanding the spirit of the law. He focused on what people should do to stay in right relationship with God, Creation, neighbor, and self.

Through parables (stories that reveal a spiritual truth), Jesus taught how the quest for right relationship enters into the most routine activities of daily life. He made God's will for humanity comprehensible, even for the less intelligent and disenfranchised members of society.

However, his talent for making the spiritual essence of the Old Testament more accessible to the people did not seem to impress the Hebrew religious leaders. They often challenged him in public, asking difficult questions in an attempt to embarrass and discredit him. Even so, they were unable to outsmart the Galilean artisan.

During one such exchange, Jesus raised the Hebrew concept of spiritual relativity to a new level when he gave an executive summary of the underlying spiritual principles of the Old Testament. In this passage from Matthew 22:34–40, Jesus affirmed that a deep capacity to love God and what God has created is the defining aspect of human spirituality:

Hearing that Jesus had silenced the Sadducees, the Pharisees got together. One of them, an expert in the law, tested him with this question: "Teacher, which is the greatest commandment in the Law?"

Jesus replied: "'Love the Lord your God with all your heart and with all your soul and with all your mind.' This is the first and greatest commandment. And the second is like it: 'Love your neighbor as yourself.' All the Law and the Prophets hang on these two commandments."

If you love God you will love what God has created—even yourself.

Jesus emphasized that a person's love for God is expressed through his or her relationships with what God has created. When an expert in the law challenged Jesus by saying, "And who is my neighbor?" Jesus didn't answer directly, but responded by telling the parable of the good Samaritan as related in Luke 10:30–37:

A man was going down from Jerusalem to Jericho, when he fell into the hands of robbers. They stripped him of his clothes, beat him and went away, leaving him half dead. A priest happened to be going down the same road, and when he saw the man, he passed by on the other side. So too, a Levite, when he came to the place and saw him, passed by on the other side. But a Samaritan, as he traveled, came where the man was; and when he saw him, he took pity on him. He went to him and bandaged his wounds, pouring on oil and wine. Then he put the man on his own donkey, took him to an inn and took care of him. The next day he took out two silver coins and gave them to the innkeeper. "Look after him," he said, "and when I return, I will reimburse you for any extra expense you may have."

Which of these three do you think was a neighbor to the man who fell into the hands of robbers?

The expert in the law replied, "The one who had mercy on him."

Jesus told him, "Go and do likewise."

For the Hebrews, this parable provided a radical view of the concept of neighbor. The priest and the Levite in the parable were obeying the letter of the law, avoiding contact with an unclean person prior to worshiping at the temple in Jerusalem. The Samaritan was the one who was a good neighbor to the wounded man—even though the Hebrews looked down upon the Samaritans for their religious beliefs.

How we act toward others is more important to God than what we believe.

Jesus taught that the concept of neighbor transcends all boundaries, just as God's love does. God's frame of reference is much more expansive than our own. God loves the whole Creation, and wants us to do the same.

Whatever God has created is your neighbor—even the dark energy.

God's love is like spiritual gravity—everything in the universe is affected by it, and it works over vast spiritual distances. Jesus showed us how to make the universe a friendly place by reflecting this love back at the Creator with gratitude and acts of compassion toward the Creation.

The Divine Dimension
· · · · ·

The kingdom of God does not come with your careful observation, nor will people say, "Here it is," or "There it is," because the kingdom of God is within you.

JESUS, LUKE 17:20–21

In many ways, Jesus had a revolutionary view of human spirituality compared with his Hebrew ancestors. While he embraced their teachings, he spoke repeatedly about something that the Old Testament does not explicitly mention: the kingdom of God (or the kingdom of heaven).

Throughout the Gospels of Mark, Matthew, and Luke, Jesus frequently talks about the good news of the kingdom of God. He says that the kingdom of God is "at hand." It is not something that exists only in the future—it is already here. It cannot be observed with the five senses—it can only be felt with the heart.

The kingdom of God is the Divine Dimension—and it's in our current space and time.

There's a very different frame of reference in the kingdom of God. This is a place where possibilities are more important than probabilities, as Jesus indicates in Luke 18:27:

What is impossible with men is possible with God.

The God formula—the equation that allows all outcomes for any situation to be possible.

The people who gain access to the kingdom of God are not necessarily the people who are successful in this world. Affluence cannot secure admission to this kingdom, as Jesus tells his disciples in Mark 10:23:

How hard it is for the rich to enter the kingdom of God!

Social status and political influence don't count for much either. In Matthew 21:21, Jesus says to the chief priests and elders of Jerusalem:

I tell you the truth, the tax collectors and the prostitutes are entering the kingdom of God ahead of you.

That remark surely had something to do with his execution.
Nevertheless, it is easy for children to enter into the kingdom of God, as Jesus emphasizes in Mark 10:14:

Let the little children come to me, and do not hinder them, for the kingdom of God belongs to such as these. I tell you the truth, anyone who will not receive the kingdom of God like a little child will never enter it.

Children understand the kingdom's wow factor and are friendly to God.
Acts of reflection and discernment also have something to do with entering the kingdom of God, as Jesus remarks to a religious leader in Mark 12:34:

When Jesus saw that he had answered wisely, he said to him, "You are not far from the kingdom of God."

This kingdom is a caring, inclusive place, where everyone rejoices when the lost one is found, as Jesus says in Luke 15:10:

There is rejoicing in the presence of the angels of God over one sinner who repents.

The good news is that the kingdom of God is a friendly place, where the human soul can stop aching and find rest and peace.

You said in your heart,
"I will ascend to heaven;
I will raise my throne
above the stars of God;
I will ascend above the
tops of the clouds;
I will make myself
like the Most High."

<small>Isaiah 14:12</small>

A place that creates spiritual supernovas rather than spiritual black holes.

Apparently, Jesus frequently interacted with the kingdom of God. But where, when, and how did this interaction take place?

According to the Gospels, Jesus often went off to be by himself, especially at night, as Mark 1:35 indicates:

> Very early in the morning, while it was still dark, Jesus got up, left the house and went off to a solitary place, where he prayed.

> *Come to me, all you who are weary and burdened, and I will give you rest. Take my yoke upon you and learn from me, for I am gentle and humble in heart, and you will find rest for your souls. For my yoke is easy and my burden is light.*
>
> JESUS, MATTHEW 11:28–30

In the clear night air of the Galilean Desert, Jesus probably looked up at the dark sky and twinkling lights above him. Maybe Jesus was an avid stargazer like his ancestor David, and enjoyed spotting his favorite constellations.

Did he like the Dippers better than all the other constellations?

As Jesus looked up, maybe he thought of David's psalms, for he was very familiar with them. Years later, Jesus quoted David's psalms while he hung on the cross dying. Beholding the night skies, perhaps Jesus recalled the lines of Psalm 8:3–4:

> When I look up at your heavens, the work of your fingers,
> The moon and the stars that you have established,
> What are human beings that you are mindful of them,
> Mortals that you care for them?

Then he probably started to pray.

That is how Jesus eased his own soul-ache, brought on by the world around him: by accessing the kingdom of God through prayer to recharge his spiritual batteries. Then he would spread God's enlightening, healing love to everyone around him—like a spiritual supernova.

A type of neutrino—call it a soultrino—flows between the Divine Dimension and the soul.

Opposite: Agave blooms tower over the Desert, often reaching heights of fifteen to twenty feet.

Jesus' ministry was dedicated to helping others make contact with the kingdom of God and experience the universe as a friendly place. He left behind plenty of clues for anyone willing to listen and learn.

Clues that help us ease our soul-ache.

Clues that can help us find spiritual security and peace in a world of instability and conflict.

Clues that can be found in the Desert.

Clues we will explore in the remaining chapters.

Frame of *Reference*	*All praise, my Lord, through Sister Earth,* *our mother who feeds us* *and gives us fruits and herbs and colored flowers.* FRANCIS OF ASSISI, *"The Canticle of Brother Sun"*

Almost two thousand years ago, Jesus proclaimed that the kingdom of God is at hand. More recently, scientists have told us that there might be more dimensions than the four we currently know about, as well as more types of neutrinos than the three we know about.

What were we thinking? That God couldn't possibly influence the universe through particles, forces, or dimensions? That we could figure out Nature, but God couldn't? We've been reaching up through the clouds and the stars to grab what belongs to God—the very same pursuit that Isaiah warned against almost three thousand years ago.

The unified theory exists in the Divine Dimension.

The twentieth-century scientist/priest Pierre Teilhard de Chardin got it right decades ago—the God of Nature and evolution (the God of the Ahead) and the God of spirituality and mysticism (the God of the Above) are one God. God's kingdom is at hand during our lives here on Earth—whether or not we understand how.

But if the kingdom of God brings good news and is here and now, why is there still so much bad news around us? Why does the dark energy of egotism, suffering, and death continue to dominate so much of human existence? Is the universe a friendly place or not? Spiritually speaking, what is going on here?

To explore these questions and find the way to spiritual security, we must carefully consider our own relationships with God, Creation, others, and self.

But what is the frame of reference that shapes our perspective on these relationships?

Would the night skies be so inspiring to us if we were like the Star Child at the end of the movie *2001: A Space Odyssey*—suspended in space, all alone in the womb, gazing out at the universe in wonder?

Fortunately, we are whizzing through space all together, snuggled up to our steadfast, nourishing mother, who holds our bodies and souls close to her with an irresistible force. While we've been looking up, she's been there all along, holding us steady so there can be an "up."

She is our frame of reference for considering our relationships with God, Creation, others, and self.

Our Mother Earth.

. . . . .

Each is not for its own sake,
I say the whole earth and all the stars in the sky are for religion's sake.
WALT WHITMAN, *"Starting from Paumanok"*

TWO

Earth

*Look to the rock from which you were hewn, and to the quarry
from which you were dug.*
ISAIAH 51:1

*You know how to interpret the appearance of the earth and the sky.
How is it that you don't know how to interpret this present time?*
JESUS, LUKE 12:56

The first man was of the dust of the earth, the second one from heaven.
PAUL, I CORINTHIANS 15:47

*Earth! you seem to look for something at my hands,
Say, old top-knot, what do you want?*
WALT WHITMAN, *"Song of Myself"*

Opposite: The summit of Picacho Peak, a landmark north of Tucson, is a chunk of
Precambrian granite over 600 million years old surrounded by younger lava remnants.

*J*une is supposed to be the hottest month here in our corner of the Sonoran Desert, and it rarely disappoints in that respect.

Even so, July and August feel much worse, regardless of what the thermometer says. Because of a change in the prevailing wind patterns, humid air and thunderstorms from the Gulf of Mexico come our way in these months. This summer rainy season is referred to as the monsoon season.

Monsoon season is a difficult time to be here. Even in early morning, the air clings to you like a desperate beggar. Late afternoon often brings dark, angry skies that are fickle about sharing their moisture. Lightning threatens to torch the Desert's parched foliage, and violent flash floods suddenly take over the roads.

Although the human population thins out considerably at this time of year, many other species enjoy the monsoon season. Any spot of water in a bowl or a fountain brings a visible parade of customers day and night: house finches, curve-billed thrashers, Gambel's quail, Gila woodpeckers, gilded flickers, rabbits, ground squirrels, packrats, mice, snakes, toads, javelinas, coyotes, and deer, to name a few. There are surely many more types of critters that come and go unobserved.

Another major reward for enduring this miserable weather is the abundance of juveniles. Since many animals reproduce in spring and early summer, July and August bring some great entertainment. Probably the most amusing juveniles are the young rabbits, with their chasing and jumping, and the young birds, with their squawking.

Juvenile birds are easy to identify for several reasons. They are continually carping and calling as a parent shows them the ropes or as they play with siblings. Their feathers are often scruffy, like a boy's cowlick.

For wildlife observation there is no better time to be here than monsoon season—although it's good to remember the "wild" aspect of wildlife.

Early one muggy morning this past July, I was sitting on the side porch with the older of my two cats, both of us avidly bird watching. After a while, he came over to sit on my lap—which he never does in hot, humid weather, given his sixteen pounds and thick silver tabby fur.

So I took him up on my lap, appreciating the feel of his fur and the sound of his purr as I stroked him and enjoyed the moment.

Suddenly, just six feet away in the Desert, I saw something large moving right in front of us. All that ran through my mind was what it wasn't: it wasn't a coyote, and it wasn't a domestic animal, and it wasn't anything I had ever seen before. My cat was disinterested in the visitor—which was also very unusual.

In an instant, my gaze was intercepted by the cool, penetrating stare of one of the Desert's top predators: a bobcat. The vast, calculating wildness in those light green eyes was unfathomable. His lanky body, just a little shorter than that of a Labrador retriever, was covered with light grayish-tan tabby fur.

It quickly became obvious that the bobcat and I shared similar thoughts: "I wasn't expecting this close encounter. But I have figured out who you are, I have kept my cool, and I am wondering what is going to happen next." I felt more awe than fear.

In addition, I imagine that this agile feline was sizing the situation up from the perspective of a hungry hunter. He had probably been attracted to my generously proportioned cat—a fact that my cat had appreciated, explaining his unusual desire to take up station on my lap. The bobcat was surely disappointed that my cat was not alone, and quickly realized that it would be too risky to jump up and try to grab him off my lap. For his part, my cat had wisely decided not to put on a territorial display, hence his seeming lack of interest in his wild feline cousin.

The bobcat also seemed to be sizing me up, not as a potential meal but as a potential threat. After about fifteen seconds of direct eye contact, which seemed to last an hour, the visitor broke off the staring contest and continued on his way.

I marveled at his easy amble, passing by as if I were the least of his concerns that morning, given the drought and the lack of food. His ears and stubby tail were striped, as if he had carefully applied black-and-white war paint before his morning rounds.

The most remarkable aspect of the encounter was that I hadn't heard anything coming. I have often heard snakes, lizards, birds, packrats, rabbits, and various other critters making their way through the Desert, despite their stealthy ways.

So how did this relatively large animal manage to get close enough to stare into my eyes without my seeing or hearing anything?

That's one of the biggest challenges of Desert living. The routine aspects of daily life easily catch your attention. Then suddenly a threat seems to come out of nowhere—like a thunderstorm blowing into the Desert during monsoon season.

Shards of Eternity
. . . . .

The dark thunder-clouds that occasionally gather over the desert seem at times to reserve all their stores of rain for one place. . . . In a very short time there is a great torrent pouring down the valley—a torrent composed of water, sand and gravel in about equal parts.
JOHN C. VAN DYKE, *The Desert*

Although most people stay away from our area during monsoon season, there are a few who enjoy visiting then, to watch the spectacular light shows that thunderstorms often bring.

One weekend in July, the weather was exceptionally hot—even for here. Moist tropical air and high temperatures hung around like annoying guests. Toward late afternoon on Sunday, clouds rose above the mountains to the east like puffy white skyscrapers.

As the sky began to darken prematurely around 5 p.m., the wind began to get nasty. The quail ran to the nearest jojoba bush for cover. The plants seemed to quiver with excitement, anticipating the welcome rain.

Then all hell broke loose. Lightning, thunder, high winds, and heavy rain pummeled the Desert for over an hour, as if the universe were mad at her. The whole sky lit up from east to west as lightning flashed, while flash floods cut through the Desert and closed several roads. The temperature dropped twenty degrees within a half hour, at least providing some relief amid the furor.

The Native Americans call the hard-driving rain typical of summer a male rain, and the gentle, soaking rain more common in winter a female rain. This was most certainly a male rain, and it did an excellent job of coaxing the creosote bushes to release their pungent aroma, as their thirsty roots soaked up the rain. It is worth a trip to the Sonoran Desert during monsoon season just to inhale that astringent, therapeutic scent.

The Desert's smell after rain helps ease the pain of a soul-ache.

The next morning the Desert looked a littler greener and the air was invigorating. The thirsty plants had probably released some extra oxygen into the air after a busy night of performing photosynthesis and sprouting new growth. Many desert-adapted plants perform photosynthesis at night using stored energy from sunlight. Since many of the Desert's plants have subtropical origins, they grow best during the hot, humid conditions of monsoon season.

Although the Desert was refreshed that morning, the roads were a mess. A load of rocky debris appeared on many roads, revealing the storm runoff's preferred routes, which are called washes. These sandy channels that flow with water only intermittently are a common feature throughout the Desert.

What is the pill which will keep us well, serene, contented? . . . Morning air! If men will not drink of this at the fountainhead of the day, why, then, we must even bottle up some and sell it in the shops, for the benefit of those who have lost their subscription ticket to morning time in the world.

HENRY DAVID THOREAU, *Walden*

Around here, runoff has been traveling through the same channels for about five million years. Each storm cuts deeper into the Desert's uppermost layer, which was deposited from five to thirteen million years ago. Once the raging water has cut through another thousand feet of Earth, the underlying volcanic rock from thirteen to twenty-two million years ago will be visible.

During monsoon season, the washes' aggressive territorial displays make you realize how easily the Desert could reclaim the roads, given half a chance.

The Desert didn't get the opportunity this time. Promptly that morning, the municipal workers came around with bulldozers and began pushing around the little shards of eternity that the rain had carried downstream.

These inconvenient rocky remnants left behind by running washes are a gentle reminder of the silent majority that rules the Desert—the mountains and the rocks.

From outer space, our terrestrial home appears as a blue, white, and green island whirling through the cosmos. These refreshing hues are formed by the large, water-rich expanses of ocean, clouds, and vegetation that cover most of the Earth's surface and help manage the global climate.

Alas, there are not any water-rich expanses of anything in the Sonoran Desert. Little rain falls here, thanks to the moisture-hogging mountain ranges to the west of us in California.

What we have here in great abundance is rocks. Anyone who doesn't like rocks should stay away, because rocks rule this Desert. From soil to sand to tiny pebbles to huge boulders to towering mountains, rocks of all ages and stages have made a home here.

Imagine the stories rocks could tell by the fire on a winter evening.

As the dominant features, mountains and rocks color the Desert's complexion with shades of cream, beige, tan, brown, red, green, gray, and black.

These are the colors in which the Earth's diary is written.

A diary that goes back billions of years.

A diary with many secrets.

A diary that is not quite finished.

According to the Earth's diary, over the past one billion years the land around here experienced massive glaciers, violent tectonic plate collisions, forceful mountain uplift, ravenous erosion, invading tropical seas, fiery volcanism, and powerful earthquakes.

Most of the mountains around here are relatively young, born between ten and fifteen million years ago. At that time, the North American plate heaved westward into the Pacific plate, creating broad valleys and exotic mountain ranges in a wide area through the Southwest known as the Basin and Range Province.

Opposite: Summer thunderstorms can make a dry wash like this run fast and furious.

Manifest destiny: go west, old plate, go west.

Mountains of varying sizes, shapes, textures, and personalities are found here in the Arizona Basin and Range territory—where friendly mountains look like temples.

Mountains with gravity.

Mountains with presence.

Mountains with attitude.

Mountains that make you stop and wonder what happened.

Each mountain has a special story. A favorite landmark around here is Black Mountain, a recovering fault with a triple peak and a split personality that stands thirty-four hundred feet high. This mountain is just a baby at thirteen million years old.

Black Mountain has seen some thirteen MILLION *sunrises over the years.*

Black Mountain was born during the Basin and Range disturbance, violently thrust up through the Earth's surface as it brought buried ancient rock along for the ride. Because this uplift occurred over a fault in the crust, the mountain's two sides look very different. The east side of the mountain is speckled with granite boulders one to two billion years old, and the older west side is cloaked in the dark metamorphic rock that makes the mountain's name so appropriate.

Forsaken of their kind, one might not inappropriately call them the "Lost Mountains"—the surviving remnant no doubt of some noble range that long centuries ago was beaten by wind and rain into desert sand.
JOHN C. VAN DYKE, *The Desert*

There was no Sonoran Desert when Black Mountain was born, since this Desert is only about eight million years old.

Just a few miles north of Black Mountain is the tallest mountain in this area, Continental Mountain, which is also about thirteen million years old. It is topped with ancient schist and quartz that is one to two billion years old.

Opposite: The south side of Black Mountain clearly reveals different rocks and terrain on each side of the fault.

Shout for joy, O heavens;

rejoice, O earth;

burst into song, O mountains!

For the Lord comforts his people

and will have compassion on his afflicted ones.

Isaiah 49:13

A mighty fortress is our God,
a bulwark never failing;
our helper he amid the flood
of mortal ills prevailing.

MARTIN LUTHER

Continental Mountain's gravity attracts the soul.

This mighty fortress stands forty-five hundred feet tall and signals the beginning of Arizona's Central Highlands. Owing to higher levels of rainfall, the north side of the mountain is covered with relatively lush chaparral vegetation rather than the sparse desert vegetation seen on the south side.

Both Black Mountain and Continental Mountain still look quite dignified, despite the latest assault on them. This time, the threat is not volcanism, earthquakes, or erosion, but a local version of "King of the Hill" in which people compete to build the highest house or housing development on the mountain by whatever means, legitimate or illegitimate.

We must seem like chump change to these mountains.

These two ancient sentinels seem to take things in stride. Why not—they know how things really work here on Earth. Sooner or later, the relentless forces of geological activity and climate change remodel every aspect of terrestrial existence like a restless homeowner.

However, the mountains can't tell us what we really want to know.

Hold old is Mother Earth, and how did she come to be as she is today?

Does she carry out these massive terrestrial remodeling projects for a reason, or out of boredom?

Does she have a bipolar personality like the rest of the universe?

Why does the Earth have living creatures while other planets apparently do not?

It's a good thing Mother Earth keeps such a thorough diary. It is from its pages that we know at least some of her life story.

Opposite: Two symbols of controversy—a roadcut and a contrail—are clearly visible near the top of Continental Mountain.

Giant Bumper Cars

. . . . .

See revolving the globe,
The ancestor-continents away group'd together,
The present and future continents north and south,
* with the isthmus between.*

WALT WHITMAN, *"Starting from Paumanok"*

From the earliest times, geological and climatic events have fascinated and frightened humanity. Today such phenomena are more comprehensible as an integral part of the Earth's unique personality.

Mother Earth is a huge, contracting, magnetic sphere that travels through space. She breathes air, dresses in water, romances the sun, and works as a master chef specializing in rocks.

Shortly after the sun formed about four and a half billion years ago, the Earth was born from a fiery collision of cosmic debris. Gravity sculpted this blazing mess of leftovers into a sphere that today measures 25,000 miles around at the equator. The moon originated from a similar collision not long after the Earth's formation.

As the Earth was formed, heavy metals such as iron and nickel sunk to the center and formed a molten core that generates a magnetic field, concentrated at the poles. This field has been particularly useful to both animals and humans in navigating vast distances.

The Earth has her own built-in way of letting us know which end is up.

Lighter elements collected in an intermediate layer (the mantle) and an outer crust (the lithosphere). Gradually the Earth cooled and contracted, and her outer crust broke into a dozen large plates and several smaller ones as well.

Although these plates lie beneath the continents and the ocean, they don't sit still, as one would think.

Instead, these tectonic plates move around on the Earth's surface and crash into one another like giant bumper cars. Their slow, forceful movements appear to be driven mainly by convective currents rising from deep within the Earth.

Is there dark energy trapped within the Earth that is trying to escape?

Where these plates come together, the Earth performs an amazing feat that appears to be unique in the cosmos. At some seams where plates adjoin, one plate tends to ride atop another, and the bottom plate is slowly reabsorbed into the molten mantle. At other seams, the mantle churns out new crust to replace what is consumed. Most of these seams lie beneath the ocean, which currently covers over 70 percent of the Earth's surface.

Every 220 million years or so, the terrestrial crust under the oceans is completely renewed through this enterprise-wide recycling program. This revitalizing process distinguishes the Earth from the moon and other planets that are barren, because it keeps the crust rich in the elements necessary for life. Our Earth is a conscientious, responsible planet, diligently working to stay nourishing to living creatures.

The Earth's self-destructive tectonic plate collisions help to sustain life.

Activity along plate junctures has often been the driving force behind mountain formation, earthquakes, volcanism, and even the movements of continents, known as continental drift.

For whatever reason, the continents that ride the terrestrial plates have an affinity for one another, and they periodically gather into one land mass. The most recent continental convention started about 225 million years ago, when all the continents drifted into one supercontinent called Pangea (Greek for "all land"), and ended about 100 million years ago as Pangea broke up. Before that, another continental convention had occurred some 800 million years ago.

In the beginning you laid the foundations
  of the earth
and the heavens are the work of your hands.
They will perish, but you remain;
they will all wear out like a garment.
Like clothing you will change them
and they will be discarded.
But you remain the same,
and your years will never end.
DAVID, PSALM 102:25–27

Such dramatic continental movements have been associated with climate change and mass extinctions on Earth. Even so, this destructive commotion has had a silver lining for life: mountains and rocks.

Just as supernovas disperse elements throughout the universe, the Earth shares these same elements through mountains, rocks, and soil. Both abundant and trace elements in the crust are important to the existence of life on Earth.

I bind unto myself today the virtues
of the starlit heaven . . .
the stable earth, the deep salt sea,
around the old eternal rocks.

"St. Patrick's Breastplate"

Most surface rocks are made from minerals derived from only a handful of elements that are plentiful in the Earth's molten interior, such as oxygen, iron, magnesium, and silicon. For example, quartz, a rock that is commonly found all over the world, is made of oxygen and silicon. Traces of calcium, sodium, potassium, and a few other elements are also widely found in the Earth's crust and in rocks.

The human body requires elements from the Earth—which are abundant in her fruits.

Here in the Desert, Mother Earth's identity cannot be concealed behind a blue, white, and green mask. She is the master chef presiding over a giant hot pot of nourishing rock stew, and her cosmic purpose is to share vital nutrients with all her children.

No matter what has happened over the past four and a half billion years, Mother Earth has just kept dishing up rocks.

Indeed, she does seem to have a bipolar personality. What appear to be self-destructive disasters to us—colliding plates, continental conventions, earth-quakes, volcanic eruptions, tidal waves, floods—are a means to her ends of making rocks and collaborating with life. Even foreign assaults by asteroids and bull-dozers are factored into her rock-making ways.

Despite all of these painstaking efforts to keep her crust nutritious, Mother Earth would be completely inhospitable to life without her protective atmospheric veil—which keeps the sun from broiling her children.

Opposite: Formed deep within the Earth and then exposed by erosion, these granite boulders are over one billion years old.

Global Village

. . . . .

The atmosphere is not a perfume, it has no taste of
  the distillation, it is odorless,
It is for my mouth forever,
I am in love with it. . . .
I am mad for it to be in contact with me.
WALT WHITMAN, *"Song of Myself"*

Although the infamous "brown cloud" of Phoenix is noxious to life, at least it reminds us that there is something that surrounds the Earth—the atmosphere.

What's in that brown cloud anyway? Will it turn black some day?

Although it's easy to forget about the atmosphere, it's not a good idea. It is Mother Earth's most important sous-chef, in charge of preparing two necessary parts of her banquet for life: air and water.

Wielding the tools of ocean and weather, the atmosphere is the one who really takes care of business here on Earth. Climatic conditions have heavily influenced almost every aspect of life, including the availability of water and food, the creation and extinction of species, the wealth of individuals and communities, and the rise and fall of civilizations.

This important terrestrial player—the atmosphere—is a layer of air, water vapor, and particles that allows plants and animals to breathe and protects them from too much sun. It contains a bio-friendly mix of nitrogen, oxygen, and a few trace gases, including carbon dioxide. Oddly enough, the sliver of carbon dioxide in the atmosphere has a major impact on the amount of solar energy that reaches the Earth's surface.

To mess with the atmosphere is to mess with self-destruction.

This defensive cover is another unique aspect of the Earth's personality, as other celestial bodies appear to have little or no atmosphere. Although the events that formed this layer are not quite clear, it appears that the atmosphere's formation was linked to the Earth's cooling and the birth of the ocean.

Mother Earth's diary confirms that the atmosphere's composition has changed dramatically over time. For over three billion years, carbon dioxide claimed a much larger share of it, which hindered the evolution of life on land. Today's oxygen level has been present in the atmosphere for less than one billion years.

Our atmosphere has several layers that stretch over 400 miles above the Earth. The two lowest levels extend about thirty miles above the surface and play a major role in weather and climate.

Humanity shares the atmosphere like a global village.

Following Mother Earth's lead with the land, the lower atmosphere likes to mix things up in the sky and the ocean. Huge masses of air and water with opposing properties keep colliding with each other, thereby redistributing important resources like solar energy and water-rich clouds. However, air and ocean currents move more at our speed over minutes and hours and days—while the land moves over thousands and millions of years.

Warm, moist air rising over heated tropical waters creates low-pressure pockets that attract cold, dry air. As a result, the steamy, heavy air of the tropics is inclined to head north to chill out, while frigid, light air from the poles rushes to the tropics to warm up— just as people and birds do!

The atmosphere is the Earth's breath—and the oceans are her lungs.

These huge air masses with contrasting humidity, temperature, and pressure engage in great pillow fights in the sky, dispersing wind, clouds, rain, hail, thunder, and lightning instead of feathers and laughs. Ocean currents, prevailing wind patterns, terrestrial features, and surface temperatures help determine where the fights will occur.

We praise you, Lord, for
  Brothers Wind and Air,
fair and stormy, all weather's moods,
by which You cherish all that You have made.
FRANCIS OF ASSISI,
"The Canticle of Brother Sun"

Lightning, a common feature of storms, is Nature's favorite way of lighting a fire on the Earth's surface—literally and figuratively! This natural source of fire has played a major role in shaping the evolution of life on Earth, clearing out old vegetation growth to make room for the new.

Fire transforms self-destructive dead wood into new life.

Since fire consumes oxygen and produces carbon dioxide, it can temporarily disrupt the local atmosphere and ecology. However, even more catastrophic changes in local atmospheric conditions have been common in the Earth's past. Mother Earth's diary reveals that incredible climatic extremes have turned the surface into a broiling furnace, a frozen wasteland, and everything in between.

Today's conditions are moderate compared to those of the past—although that might be changing.

Along with the sun and the moon, the Earth's land, ocean, atmosphere, and biosphere shape the climate in ways that are still not fully understood.

While this climatic partnership is beyond our current comprehension, it is not beyond our influence. Over the past hundred years, a general climatic warming trend has been accelerating owing to the presence in the air of increased amounts of gases like carbon dioxide, partly if not wholly the result of industrial activity and vehicle exhaust.

Can the universe be a friendly place if we make the Earth uninhabitable?

Maybe the clear and present danger of global warming will finally teach us that, when it comes to the Earth, humanity can easily stake a claim but cannot call the shots for long. Land, water, fire, and air belong to Mother Earth, not to us.

Just as the mountains and rocks have known all along.

Unfortunately, we are learning this lesson the hard way, like so many others before us.

Others like the ancient Hebrews.

The Promised Land ·····	*"Heaven is my throne, and the earth is my footstool. . . .* *Has not my hand made all these things, and so they came into being?"* *declares the Lord.* ISAIAH 66:1–2

About ten thousand years ago, the last ice age ended. As temperatures, rainfall, and flooding moderated, permanent agricultural settlements proliferated. The local climate and growing conditions became the source of everything that sustains life.

This new partnership with the Earth deeply affected the physical, emotional, intellectual, and spiritual dimensions of human life. The agrarian lifestyle brought several important changes to human society, including a sense of connection to a place, the concept of owning land, and more intense territorial disputes.

As an agrarian people, the ancient Hebrews had a close relationship with the Earth. Even though they probably didn't know that similar elements are found in both the Earth's crust and the human body, they intuitively understood that the Earth and human beings are intimately linked.

There's something of the Earth in us—and there's something of us in the Earth.

They had a holistic view of the relationships between God, the Earth, and humanity. Desirable conditions—such as adequate rain, sunshine, and successful crops—led to abundance, physical nutrition, and contentment for the whole clan, and so were associated with divine approval of human activities. Likewise, detrimental events—such as drought and flood—led to scarcity, illness, and death and so were considered signs of divine disapproval of the community.

About four thousand years ago, Abram (later to be named Abraham), one of the earliest Hebrew leaders, set out from his home with the hope of settling in another place based on his covenant with God. After an extended sojourn, Abraham settled on the outskirts of Canaan, a fertile area in the Middle East.

In the covenant, or deal, between God and Abraham, God promised descendants and land to Abraham, and asked for loyalty and obedience in return. Abraham and his descendants were to be the people of God, and not worship other gods.

For Abraham's descendants, God's request proved to be challenging. As did other Middle Eastern people of the time, the Hebrews believed that minor gods (called baals) accounted for the differences in the crop productivity of various fields. These baals needed to be appeased to ensure successful crops.

> *By the sweat of your face*
> *you shall eat bread*
> *until you return to the ground,*
> *for out of it you were taken;*
> *you are dust,*
> *and to dust you shall return.*
> GOD TO ADAM, GENESIS 3:19

As a result, the seed of monotheism planted by Abraham grew slowly. For several centuries after the covenant had been made, many Hebrews worshiped God *and* the baals, rather than God alone. This situation might account for the use of a plural form of the word for God (*elohim*) in some early parts of Genesis.

I will establish my covenant between me and you...for an everlasting covenant, to be God to you and to your offspring after you. And I will give to you, and to your offspring after you, the land where you are now an alien, all the land of Canaan, for a perpetual holding; and I will be their God.

GOD TO ABRAHAM,
GENESIS 17:7–8 NRSV

During a period of drought about thirty-six hundred years ago, many of Abraham's descendants migrated to the south and ended up in Egypt. Eventually they were enslaved by the Egyptians and lived in captivity for about three hundred years. Through divine intervention and the leadership of Moses, they left Egypt around 1250 BC and wandered in the Middle Eastern Desert for forty years.

During this aimless period, the Hebrews yearned for a patch of land to call their own. They recalled the abundant land that had been promised to Abraham by God, land that held the hope of physical, emotional, and spiritual security. It was a place where they would have enough to eat and drink and could settle down, increase their numbers and territory, and freely practice their religion.

The anticipated material benefits of the Promised Land are described by Moses in Deuteronomy 8:7–9:

> For the Lord your God is bringing you into a good land, a land flowing with streams, with springs and underground waters welling up in valleys and hills, a land of wheat and barley, a land of vines and fig trees and pomegranates, a land of olive trees and honey, a land where you may eat bread without scarcity, where you will lack nothing, a land whose stones are iron and from whose hills you may mine copper.

Opposite: Like the Promised Land, the upper Sonoran Desert enjoys a rugged yet abundant landscape.

Be still, and know that I am God;

I will be exalted among the nations,

I will be exalted in the earth.

<small>Psalm 46:10</small>

However, the Promised Land was not just to be for good times and economic gain. Moses made it clear that the Hebrews had to fulfill their part of the deal with God—to love and obey God alone—in order to gain and keep the Promised Land. Baal worship, or idolatry, was a violation of the covenant.

Before the Hebrews left the Desert, God gave Moses a set of moral guidelines to help them understand how to fulfill their part of the covenant. With fear and trembling, Moses received the Ten Commandments on Mount Sinai and wrote them on stone tablets.

The Ten Commandments formed a clear, cogent moral code that was unprecedented in the world at that time. As Deuteronomy 5:6–21 indicates, this code gives guidelines for right relationship with God (commandments 1–3) and right relationship with other people (commandments 4–10):

1. I am the Lord your God, who brought you out of bondage, out of the land of slavery. You shall have no other gods but me.
2. You shall not make for yourself an idol in the form of anything in heaven above or on the earth beneath or in the waters below.
3. You shall not misuse the Name of the Lord your God.
4. Observe the Sabbath day by keeping it holy.
5. Honor your father and your mother.
6. You shall not murder.
7. You shall not commit adultery.
8. You shall not steal.
9. You shall not give false testimony against your neighbor.
10. You shall not covet your neighbor's wife. You shall not set your desire on your neighbor's house or land, his manservant or maidservant, his ox or donkey, or anything that belongs to your neighbor.

Moses warned the Hebrews to live by the covenant and keep God's commandments in order to enter and keep the Promised Land, as Deuteronomy 30:19–20 confirms:

I call heaven and earth to witness against you today that I have set before you life
and death, blessings and curses. Choose life so that you and your descendants
may live, loving the Lord your God, obeying him . . . so that you may live in the
land that the Lord swore to give your ancestors, to Abraham, to Isaac, and to
Jacob.

Shortly thereafter, Moses died. Under the leadership of Joshua, the Hebrews
engaged in several violent conflicts (described in chapters 6–12 of the book of
Joshua) to conquer the land of Canaan west of the Jordan River. When the
Hebrews invaded the city of Jericho, their conquest was heartless and thorough, as
Joshua 6:21 NRSV relates:

Then they devoted to destruction by the edge of the sword all in the city, both men
and women, young and old, oxen, sheep, and donkeys.

Ultimately they prevailed over the previous inhabitants, the Canaanites, and settled in this land.

Given the favor that God had shown to the Hebrews by miraculously delivering
them from Egypt, it seems contradictory that they should have had to struggle so
fiercely to take hold of the land that was promised to Abraham under the covenant.

Was this really what God wanted? For the people of God to spend their time fighting and killing
to enter the Promised Land? For God's people to
relate to the Earth as a treasure to be possessed, a
sponge to sop up blood?

> *The earth will disclose the*
> *blood shed upon her;*
> *she will conceal her slain no longer.*
> ISAIAH 26:21

What about the sixth commandment—"You
shall not murder"? Was it acceptable to kill the occupants of the Promised Land,
or had something gotten lost in their interpretation of God's will?

Did they eventually lose the land over the blood that was spilled on it?

What about the tenth commandment—"You shall not covet anything that
belongs to your neighbor"—including land? Did the non-Hebrew peoples around
them not count as neighbors?

Who really "owned" the Promised Land? Who "owns" it now?

Did they or did they not break God's commandments? Was the Promised Land a reward for obeying God's commandments, or the spoils won by breaking them?

Despite Moses' earlier warning, the Old Testament documents a history of idolatry and bloodshed among the Hebrews during their twelve hundred years in the Promised Land. Somehow, somewhere, things went way off track in the relationships among God, the Hebrews, their neighbors, and the Promised Land.

Apparently, the Hebrews' desire for the Promised Land's material rewards overshadowed their spiritual commitment to the covenant with God.

The human struggle to balance economic concerns with spiritual priorities is an ancient one, and it continues to this day for everyone alive. But when it came to recording the dimensions of this struggle, the ancient Hebrews wrote the book.

For all humanity, and for all time. At least as far as Jesus was concerned.

We are all the people of God.

Paradise *Regained*	*But I tell you, do not swear at all: either by heaven, for it is God's throne; or by the earth, for it is his footstool.* JESUS, MATTHEW 5:24–25

Once the Hebrews had settled in the Promised Land of Palestine, life was never dull. After the reigns of David and Solomon had ended by 930 BC, political instability and invasions became common. The Hebrews endured frequent and numerous military conflicts, as such neighboring nations as Babylonia, Assyria, Egypt, and Greece swept through the strategically important Middle East.

By the time the Romans showed up around 50 BC, the Hebrews were as receptive to foreigners as the crusty residents of a tourist town are to the "summer folk."

Several decades later, Jesus was born in the Promised Land. At that time, the leaders of the Hebrews and the representatives of the Roman Empire maintained an uneasy coexistence, each side resistant to the other's ways.

Although he was born in Bethlehem, Jesus spent most of his life in the nearby farming village of Nazareth, a part of Galilee renowned for its fertile ground and mild climate. During his lifetime, Galileans grew a great variety of crops, including herbs, grains, and vegetables, and maintained vineyards as well as groves of olive, fruit, and fig trees.

Jesus must have known the sweet smell of citrus blossoms gently warmed by the Galilean sun.

Galileans had a particular accent and were considered plain country people, since they lived close to the land and were a bit lax in their religious practices.

Even Jesus had a hard time getting through to them, as he indicates in Mark 6:4:

Prophets are not without honor, except in their hometown, and among their own kin, and in their own house.

Nevertheless, these simple, humble folk were a major part of the target market he intended to reach with his radical new message about the kingdom of God.

While Jesus' first thirty years are somewhat obscure, the Gospels of Matthew and Luke indicate that he came from a devout Hebrew family descended from the House of David, and worked with his father as an artisan, building with wood and stone.

A hands-on, outdoorsy kind of occupation.

At the age of thirty he began his public ministry, traveling primarily through the towns of Galilee and the city of Jerusalem, healing and teaching everywhere he went.

Another hands-on, outdoorsy kind of occupation.

He probably came off as a bit of a rube in the larger towns and cities, with his funny accent, good tan, well-worn clothes, lean body, dusty feet, calloused hands, gentle eyes, and tender-hearted message.

And that smile. That broad, soul-warming smile.

Maybe that's why many rejected him. As one skeptic said in John 1:46:

Can anything good come out of Nazareth?

However, he seemed to say something of great value, as crowds gathered around him often during his three-year ministry.

During his youth in the bountiful rolling hills of Galilee, Jesus certainly absorbed a deep appreciation for the Earth. Throughout all four gospels, there are various descriptions of how he interacted with the Earth.

On one occasion, the scribes and Pharisees (the religious elites of the time) gathered to stone a prostitute—the legal remedy for her sin. But before going ahead with the punishment, they asked for Jesus' opinion, hoping to trap him as a lawbreaker. As John 8:6–8 indicates, his response was unusual:

The stone that the builders rejected has become the chief cornerstone. This is the Lord's doing; It is marvelous in our eyes.

PSALM 118:22–23

> Jesus bent down and wrote with his finger on the ground. When they kept on questioning him, he straightened up and said to them, "Let anyone among you who is without sin be the first to throw a stone at her." And once again he bent down and wrote on the ground.

Jesus touched the ground to gain insight, and stood aligned with the Earth to possess strength. Some ancient versions of the Bible even indicate that Jesus was writing the sins of the woman's accusers on the ground.

He could somehow understand people from the inside out—just as God does.

Jesus used the Earth to heal people, as indicated in this passage from John 9:11 quoting a man born blind:

> The man called Jesus made mud, spread it on my eyes, and said to me, "Go to Siloam and wash." Then I went and washed and received my sight.

Earth, water, the human body, and faith complete a circuit with the Divine Dimension.

Jesus considered a patch of Earth an integral part of the people who lived on it, as indicated in this instruction to his disciples in Mark 6:11:

> If any place will not welcome you and they refuse to hear you, as you leave, shake off the dust that is on your feet as a testimony against them.

The Earth played a leading role in one of Jesus' greatest miracles—the only miracle recorded in all four gospels. Before feeding five thousand people with but five loaves of bread and two fish, he had everyone sit on the ground, as recounted in Mark 6:39:

> Then he ordered them [his disciples] to get all the people to sit down in groups on the green grass.

Was he somehow able to convert energy into matter by connecting everyone with the Earth?

And his special relationship with the Earth was not limited to dry land. In Mark 6:45–52, the miracle of the loaves and fish is immediately followed by a story about Jesus' walking on water toward the disciples' boat during a storm, which subsides once he arrives and tells them to not be afraid.

Another story related in the Gospels of Matthew, Mark, and Luke tells how Jesus was with his disciples in a boat when a storm came up, and responded to their distress in this way (Mark 6:39–40):

> He woke up and rebuked the wind and said to the sea, "Peace! Be still!" Then the wind ceased, and there was a dead calm. He said to them, "Why are you afraid? Have you still no faith?"

Did soultrinos enable him to manage energy like that?

Ultimately, Jesus saw the Earth as part of the family of God, ready to fulfill the divine will even if people would not. On his triumphant entry into Jerusalem, when the envious Pharisees suggested that he order his disciples to stop their praises, Luke 19:40 tells us that he answered:

> I tell you, if these were silent, the stones would shout out.

We praise and bless You, Lord,
*   and give You thanks,*
and serve You in all humility.
Francis of Assisi,
The Canticle of Brother Sun

Jesus lived close to the land. Close to the humus. He was humble. Full of humility, and fully human.

The press of my foot to the earth springs a hundred affections
They scorn the best I can do to relate them.

<small>WALT WHITMAN, *"Song of Myself"*</small>

Humble, humility, human. All from the Latin word *humus*, meaning Earth or soil, which in turn is derived from the ancient Indo-European word for Earth.

Humility attracts the Divine Dimension as a magnet attracts iron.

Jesus understood what it is to be in right relationship with the Earth. However, his message clearly indicated that the land beneath our feet is not the territory that matters most.

The Earth is a means to an end, a pathway to what matters most—the Promised Land of the heart.

The Promised Land is not beneath us, but within us.

The Promised Land is the very ground of being that sustains the human soul.

The Promised Land is in God's territory—the kingdom of heaven.

God's territory needs to increase—not ours.

Jesus taught that the Promised Land within us can be taken away only with our consent, no matter what happens to the ground beneath our feet.

Paradise is a moveable feast. You can find it while you are here—and you *can* take it with you.

---

what the Earth wants
· · · · ·

No politics, song, religion, behavior, or what not, is of account,
Unless it compare with the amplitude of the earth,
Unless it face the exactness, vitality, impartiality,
    rectitude of the earth.
WALT WHITMAN, *"A Song of the Rolling Earth"*

Given the obvious love and respect for the Earth at the center of Jesus' teachings, it is difficult to understand why the United States and other countries, whose citizens and leaders are still predominantly Christian, have been treating the Earth like a commercial commodity for centuries.

Like spoiled children betraying their mother.

As industrialization took hold in the eighteenth and nineteenth centuries, the

Opposite: A popular hiking path keeps track of visitors.

Earth was increasingly viewed as just another resource to be exploited in the formula for determining profits: land, labor, capital, and entrepreneurship.

Just like old times in the Promised Land.

The industrial capacity that helped the United States win World War II and become an economic superpower also spurred an exodus from the countryside to the cities. As fewer and fewer people lived close to the land, it became easy to forget that the Earth provides both physical and spiritual sustenance to us.

Are we giving Mother Earth a soul-ache?

The development of plate tectonic theory and that famous photograph of the Earth sent home by the American astronauts on July 21, 1969, began to change our frame of reference. Both scientists and astronauts have made us aware of how unique and fragile our terrestrial home really is from a cosmic perspective.

Since the first Earth Day on April 21, 1971, all sorts of celebrations, meetings, and summits regarding the Earth have been held all over the world, marking a renewed interest in the bounty and beauty of our planet.

After decades of research, analysis, and discussion, we can finally appreciate Mother Earth for what she is: the friendly ambassador of life in a hostile, barren universe.

From our frame of reference, she is a great globe of grace—an unearned blessing.

She continues to do so much for us. Perhaps there is something we can do for her.

In one of this chapter's opening quotes, Walt Whitman asked what the Earth wants.

Surely he knew that the Earth wants what every mother wants: she wants to be loved.

For this Earth,
She lives with no other thought
Than to love and be loved
By we.

She wants to be loved—and she wants us to get along with her other children.

For if you love Mother Earth, you must be humble enough, and human enough, to love her children—ALL her children, human or not—as well as the air, water, and land that sustain them.

Mother Earth is always looking out for us. She knows the truth better than we do—the universe could never be a friendly place if we were all alone on this planet.

．　．　．　．　．

He who created the heavens, he is God;
he who fashioned and made the earth, he founded it;
he did not create it to be empty, but formed it to be inhabited.
ISAIAH 45:18

THREE

Life

Holy, holy, holy is the Lord of hosts;
The whole earth is full of his glory.
Isaiah 6:3

Which of you fathers, if your son asks for a fish, will give him a snake instead?
Or if he asks for an egg, will give him a scorpion?
Jesus, Luke 11:11–12

For the creation waits with eager longing for the revealing of the children of God.
We know that the whole creation has been groaning in labor pains until now.
Paul, Romans 8:19–22

God has made all things that are made; and God loves all that he has made.
Julian of Norwich, *Revelation of Love*

Opposite: A startled rattlesnake gets ready to strike in self-defense.

For many people, the word *desert* conjures up the image of a vast, barren, windswept expanse of sand with few inhabitants. A desert appears to be a place deserted by almost everyone, a forlorn wilderness that lacks abundance.

Even though the world's deserts vary greatly in terms of climate, biota, and terrain, they are defined by one common feature: exceptional dryness. A desert can be hot or cold, but it usually has ten or fewer inches of rain per year and low humidity.

This extreme aridity presents a high-stakes survival challenge to anything that needs water to live—which is everything that lives. Deserts are not usually teeming with life.

But here in the Sonoran Desert, things are a little different.

At just over eight million years old, the Sonoran Desert is a mere child among the biotic communities covering the Earth's surface, born like the others of geological activity and climate change.

However, her genetic ancestry goes back almost fifty million years to the tropical forests and animals that easily traveled up through Central America to invade North America during wetter times.

Because of this deep connection to the tropics, the Sonoran Desert today enjoys a generous level of biodiversity. With over thirty-five hundred species of plants, over eight hundred species of vertebrates, and unknown thousands of arthropod species, this is the most vital desert in the world.

Here in the foothills of the upper Sonoran Desert, we receive an average of fourteen inches of rainfall annually—so technically this area is not even a desert. This supplemental water is put to good use by the Desert, giving our area an extra helping of plants and wildlife.

So you never know whom you might run across.

None of the brute creation requires more than Food and Shelter. . . .
Food may be regarded as the Fuel which keeps up the fire within us.
. . . The grand necessity, then, for our bodies, is to keep warm, to
keep the vital heat in us.
HENRY DAVID THOREAU, *Walden*

One mild spring Saturday morning, when we returned home around 9 a.m. there was a snake lying across the side of our gravel driveway. We spied her late, so I wasn't sure if we might have run her over. She didn't move, so I went over to see if we had injured her.

She was a friendly-looking snake, pale yellow with subtle brown and tan racing stripes and a very long tail that tapered to a fine point. Her head was rounded and narrow, unlike the large triangular head of a rattler. She didn't appreciate the attention and slowly slid under a jojoba bush, as if to demonstrate that all her parts were in working order.

About five minutes later, looking out the kitchen window, I noticed a strange lump of something right in the middle of the driveway, not far from where the snake had been. Because of a visible light stripe, it looked like a ground squirrel that was twisted into an impossible position.

So I went to check things out. On closer examination, it appeared to be the same snake we had seen earlier, coiled in a ball with her shiny buff-colored belly forming the "stripe" I had seen. Every now and then her tail thrashed about wildly and her sides convulsed.

Perhaps she was trying to shed her skin. But snakes usually attend to such personal hygiene rituals in protected areas such as under a bush. She was in a highly vulnerable position, but seemed undisturbed by my presence.

There was a young lizard about six feet away from the snake, going along a nearby split-rail fence and stopping every few inches as if to look for something he had lost.

I left for about ten minutes and then returned to a bizarre sight. The snake was no longer in a ball, but had spread out into a loose arc, and it appeared to have no head but two tails! Once I got within six feet, the mystery was solved.

This snake had been coiled atop an adult lizard, and had literally been snuffing the daylights out of the poor thing while I was watching. The thrashing tail that I thought was the snake's had actually belonged to the lizard. The snake's convulsing sides reflected the lizard's desperate attempts to escape this scaly tomb.

Now the hapless herp, probably an adult whiptail lizard, appeared to be quite dead, having been pulled head first into the snake's mouth. So that's why it looked as if the snake had two tails—most of the lizard's body and tail were sticking out of the snake's mouth!

Every so often, the snake's sides contracted, and a little more of the lizard's body disappeared. It was amazing that such a small snake could wolf down a lizard of that size. Her mouth was open very wide.

Both repulsed and mesmerized, I stood watching. Then another spectator came along—the little lizard that had been looking for something earlier along the fence. He stood about three feet away from the snake, intently observing the grisly feast. It occurred to me that perhaps he was wondering what his mother was doing sticking out of that snake's mouth.

After the adult lizard was almost totally consumed, Junior darted off alone into the Desert.

We think reptiles don't have emotions—hopefully they don't.

Just then, about twelve feet down the driveway, a large collared lizard sauntered out of a bush onto the driveway to catch some rays.

Collared lizards supposedly don't eat snakes, but they do eat lizards. Maybe he would go for the two-for-one special that the full snake offered. The stuffed snake would be slow and vulnerable after such a feast on a warm morning.

In the Desert, what goes around comes around. The little orphan's recent loss would be avenged sooner or later.

They are all just trying to keep their vital heat going—but why is Nature so cruel?

As I later found out, the agile predator that had consumed the lizard was a western patchnose snake, named for a hard spot on the snake's nose that assists it in burrowing for reptile eggs. The patchnose is not a constrictor, as I had suspected. It subdues its prey by pressing coils of its body over the victim until suffocation occurs.

Perhaps when we originally drove up the driveway that lovely spring morning, the mother lizard was showing her teenager the ropes of Desert life. When the patchnose snake slithered under the jojoba bush, she probably interrupted the pair's hunting class and pursued Mama up the driveway. The patchnose must have moved at the speed of light, because the lizards here are incredibly fast.

Then the snake tackled Mama on the driveway where I found them, and proceeded to suffocate and consume her right before Junior and me.

At least Mama's genes live on in Junior. That's her consolation prize.

Is there a consolation prize in life other than passing on our genes?

There is no living in concord or brotherhood here. Everything is at war with its neighbor, and the conflict is unceasing. Yet this conflict is not so obvious on the face of things. You hear no clash or crash or snarl. The desert is overwhelmingly silent.
JOHN C. VAN DYKE, *The Desert*

Most people out here have never heard of a patchnose snake. There's only one snake in this Desert that anyone pays much attention to.

The snake everyone loves to hate.

The snake with enough poisonous venom to kill a person.

The rattlesnake.

*There is, however, only one reptile on the desert that humanity need greatly fear on account of his poison and that is the rattlesnake.
. . . He is not a pleasant creature, but then he is not often met with.*
JOHN C. VAN DYKE, *The Desert*

Animal House
. . . . .

The Sonoran Desert is home to a generous collection of snakes that includes more species of rattlesnakes than any other region in the world, including the western diamondback, Mohave, tiger, and blacktail rattlesnakes and the sidewinder.

Around here the western diamondback rattler is the most common type. This fierce predator is not inclined to be messed with by curious onlookers, and will strike with or without warning, especially when cornered.

However, most snakebites can be attributed to a dangerous combination of

testosterone and alcohol—when drunken men handle rattlers in an ill-advised fit of bravado. Rattlers are infamous for "biting" up to an hour after they're dead—behavior that can catch anyone off guard, drunk or sober.

But when rattlers really want to do some damage, it's not people that they're after.

Toward dusk one hot evening in early August, we were walking from the back-yard into the house when we were stopped by an unmistakable sound. It was something like the hissing noise an irrigation system makes when the water first starts to flow.

We knew the sound all too well. There was a rattlesnake under a bush about four feet away, and he was mad that we had breeched his territory. We backed up and retreated, glad that he had rattled before striking.

Above: A squiggly line thought to represent a snake is a common feature of Hohokam rock art in the area.

He must have come to that spot very recently, because he hadn't been there just a few minutes earlier. He had probably been getting into position to hunt that night. But what was he after so near our house? Neither humans nor cats make suitable prey for a rattler.

Then it occurred to me that he was after whoever had been leaving behind bundles of excrement on our back porch at night, most likely a packrat.

About a half hour after our sudden encounter, it was almost dark. I looked out at the bush where the snake had been. He was on the move to another bush even closer to the back porch, full of menace. Rattlers are highly skilled at locating prey by sensing heat and movement, so he was now in a good position to strike at something on the back porch with minimal movement or warning.

The next morning, I could see that the rattler's hunting strategy had been successful. Under a bush, he was stretched out against the cool foundation of our house with a huge bulge in his sleek body.

There is a war of elements and a struggle for existence going on here that for ferocity is unparalleled elsewhere in nature. The feeling of fierceness grows upon you as you come to know the desert better.

JOHN C. VAN DYKE, *The Desert*

Imagine the packrat's surprise when he arrived at our back porch and was greeted by the rattler's sudden pounce. The snake's venom did the trick, paralyzing the hapless rodent so the rattler could easily swallow him whole.

Did the packrat know what was coming? Did he suffer?

Weighed down by his plunder, the snake looked like he was staying put for a while. So we named him Ricky, and kept tabs on him as a precaution and out of curiosity. Each day the shrinking bulge kept moving down Ricky's body, but Ricky himself didn't move.

One very hot morning three days after the murder, Ricky finally came out of his hiding place. Having regained his trim, muscular form, he was ready to go on the prowl again.

We were at the side of the house doing some chores when Ricky slithered by. He passed only about six feet away from us without rattling, as if he had gotten used to us just as we had gotten used to him. We watched as he slowly slithered around the base of a stone wall, looking for an opening between the cool rocks. Then he found one, and tried to wiggle in.

Something strange happened next.

Ricky thrust the front half of his body into the crevice, so that the back half with the rattle was all we could see. Then his head came out on the other side of the rock, but his midsection was still obscured by the rock.

There he was, head and tail sticking out from the wall, apparently unconnected. He stayed like that for about a minute as we watched from nearby; then he extricated himself from the wall and meandered out into the Desert.

Ricky's farewell stunt was a good reminder of how things really work in the Desert: everything is interconnected—whether or not it appears to be.

The packrats fear the rattler. The rattlers fear the king snake, their archenemy, known to sometimes eat a rattler that is still alive. They all fear the Harris hawk, a neotropical raptor adept at snatching a wide variety of fast-moving prey.

In turn, the Harris hawk is done in by poachers and the electrical lines it encounters atop utility poles.

We're all stalked by the dark energy of fear and death.

All the members of the Desert's community of life are interdependent, whether or not we understand the connection. No species is superfluous—life is too hard for anyone to live here without a purpose.

The several thousand species that call the Sonoran Desert home are but a drop in the bucket of the world's biodiversity. An estimated ten to one hundred million species currently inhabit the Earth—an astonishing array of life that makes you wonder how it all came to be.

After the Earth's fiery birth, how did life begin? What challenges did life meet as it evolved into the prolific family of species that exists today?

Have sexual reproduction and predation always played central roles in the game of life—or are they more recent developments?

Opposite: The Harris hawk adapted to the harsh conditions of the Sonoran Desert through an unusual group-hunting approach to predation.

The spotted hawk swoops by and accuses me,

he complains of my gab and my loitering.

I too am not a bit tamed, I too am untranslatable,

I sound my barbaric yawp over the roofs of the world.

WALT WHITMAN, *"Song of Myself"*

Why are there so many species alive today? Given how many there are, does it matter if human activity expedites the extinction process for some of them?

The Desert does not have the answers to these questions, but she can help point us in the right direction. When the wind blows the right way, even here in the Desert there's a smell in the air that reminds us of where it all began.

Our "country of origin."

Mother Earth's womb of life.

The ocean.

In the Beginning
. . . . .

I have called this principle, by which each slight variation, if useful, is preserved, by the term Natural Selection.
CHARLES DARWIN, *The Origin of Species*

Life on Earth started with a whimper, not a bang.

For more than three billion years, life on Earth never advanced beyond single-celled organisms living in the ocean. Eventually life evolved beyond microscopic organisms, invaded dry land, and produced the bountiful biodiversity that surrounds us today.

Throughout its history, life has been struggling to reconcile the same forces that govern the universe—collaboration and self-destruction.

Almost four billion years ago, the terrestrial surface had cooled off somewhat. In the ocean—most likely in a tidal pool or at a thermal vent on the ocean floor— heat, water, and minerals collaborated to form the first single cell through a process that scientists have thus far not been able to replicate.

Life began on the edge where somethingness meets otherness.

Somehow or another, this first organism figured out how to eat and stay alive. From the beginning, this need to consume resources to fuel metabolism has forced living creatures to interact with their environment—and to live at its mercy.

To be alive is to be at risk for not having enough resources.

In addition, early life figured out how to reproduce asexually and give its offspring survival instructions through genes. The most useful combinations of genes allowed some organisms to survive better than others and pass these successful genes on.

To be alive is to share one's self and help others.

Things must have gone pretty well for early life. For over three billion years, simple organisms ruled the seas, reproducing asexually and proliferating in marine colonies. Although they were unchallenged by other life forms, they experienced extremely hostile environmental conditions.

Somewhere along the line, these microbes encountered a major threat, not from the environment, but from within the colony itself. Thanks to a reproductive error, a good cell went bad and turned into a selfish "cheater cell," consuming excessive resources and engaging in uncontrolled growth. This self-destructive behavior is still evident today in cells that become cancerous and form tumors.

A self-destructive cheater cell consumes too much for fear of not having enough.

However, life figured out how to work around the cheater cell's selfish ways.

About one billion years ago, aerobic multicellular organisms evolved in the ocean as oxygen levels increased. Individual cells started to perform more specialized tasks, such as metabolism, respiration, and reproduction, with all cells working together for the benefit of the organism.

Collaboration for the benefit of the whole—the miracle of multicellular life.

These more complex multicellular organisms laid the genetic groundwork for new behaviors, including predation and sexual reproduction.

Why did living creatures have to start eating each other?

Sexual reproduction allows for improved accuracy in replicating genes, and makes the inheritance of any given gene a possibility rather than a certainty, since offspring can receive genes from either parent.

This bell-curve approach to genetic inheritance keeps deviant yet prolific cheater cells from taking over the gene pool. Variety is not just the spice of life—it is the protector of life.

The purpose of life is to outwit cheater cells.

Then it happened—the equivalent of the Big Bang for life on Earth.

Left Behind
. . . . .

Over 550 million years ago, the ocean exploded with many new types of animals. Called the Cambrian event, this unprecedented growth spurt finally introduced creatures large enough to be visible to the naked eye. These were the early ancestors of all animals alive today—including humans.

However, the journey from the Cambrian event to today's biodiversity has not been an easy one. Catastrophic extinctions have played a major role in shaping the family tree of life on Earth.

While Charles Darwin dismissed mass extinctions as fantastic stories with no scientific basis, additional findings have proven him dead wrong on this issue.

Nature has used the "unnatural selection" of devastating extinction events to topple the winners of the natural selection game. Genes successful under typical conditions are not always useful to survival when conditions dramatically change.

Dark energy keeps trying to destroy life through genetic defects and mass extinctions.

However, no matter how bad things got during past extinction events, there was always a remnant of survivors that kept life going so that we could be here today.

I love to see that Nature is so rife with life that myriads can be afforded to be sacrificed and suffered to prey on one another; that tender organizations can be so serenely squashed out of existence like pulp . . . and that sometimes it has rained flesh and blood!

HENRY DAVID THOREAU, *Walden*

Since the Cambrian event, five major extinctions have occurred that destroyed at least 70 percent of all living species. Changes in sea level, climate change, and asteroid impacts are some of the suspects behind these cataclysmic events. Yet each of these disasters has introduced new opportunities for the survivors.

Dark energy loves to cause mass extinctions, so soultrinos use them to help life along.

About 440 million years ago, a major extinction hit marine life particularly hard, possibly caused by a massive volcanic eruption following an asteroid impact.

Relatively soon thereafter, life finally ventured out of the ocean, as primitive plants and arthropods began to live on land. It had taken life over three billion years to crawl out of the sea.

Land plants ate sunshine for a living, and insects ate plants and each other.

Some 75 million years later, another major extinction of indeterminate causes occurred. Soon after, tropical forests and amphibians proliferated on the receptive land. Then the first reptiles appeared, descended from amphibians but better equipped for terrestrial life.

About 300 million years ago, as climate change urged deserts to replace tropical forests throughout the Earth, insects proliferated. Mammal-like reptiles evolved amid the sand dunes, successfully dominating terrestrial life for the next 80 million years. Small mammals quickly evolved from these mammal-like reptiles, but remained minor players in terrestrial life for almost 250 million years thereafter, inhibited by the presence of dinosaurs.

Reptiles, insects, and mammals go way back with the Desert.

Over 225 million years ago, the greatest catastrophe of all time hit the biosphere. As the continents gradually coalesced into the supercontinent Pangea and volcanism raged, two major extinctions occurred in relatively quick succession.

How long did the smell of death pollute the atmosphere?

This Permian-Triassic (P-T) extinction event wiped out some 95 percent of all marine and terrestrial species, probably because of reduced oxygen levels in the ocean and in the air. As shallow seas flooded deserts, mammal-like reptiles were destroyed, but dinosaurs thrived and went on to dominate the Earth for the next 140 million years.

Could WE possibly avoid self-destruction for 140 million years?

Within 50 million years of the P-T extinction event, birds evolved from feathered reptiles that glided between trees in pursuit of food. Encouraged by avian pollinators, more complex flowering plants and hardwood forests began to proliferate over 100 million years ago.

Photosynthesis and pollination reflect the universe's collaborative streak.

About 65 million years ago, the most recent mass extinction occurred after a huge asteroid several miles wide apparently collided with the Earth near the Yucatán Peninsula. This impact produced a giant tidal wave and a thick layer of dust that caused the fastest extinction on record, known as the Cretaceous-Tertiary (K-T) event.

With photosynthesis blocked by the clogged atmosphere, plants quickly perished, disrupting the entire food chain. Almost 70 percent of all marine and land animal species died off within a few months, and dinosaurs quickly became extinct.

And as to you Death, you bitter hug of mortality, it is idle to try to alarm me.
WALT WHITMAN, *"Song of Myself"*

Were dinosaurs too high-maintenance to survive, owing to their large appetites?

But the dinosaurs' loss was our gain. When life bounced back, our small, shrewlike ancestors flourished, leading mammals to play a more significant role in the drama of terrestrial life.

Over the past 60 million years, the number of species has rebounded to the estimated ten to one hundred million species living today. Unfortunately, fewer than four million of those species have even been identified.

Of these known species, approximately 70 percent are animals, 25 percent are higher plants, and 5 percent are microbes, algae, and fungi. Over three-fourths of the known animal species are arthropods, such as insects, spiders, and crustaceans, and fewer than 1 percent are mammals.

Perversely, the biotic groups we consider the least intelligent—such as microbes, fungi, plants, arthropods, amphibians, and reptiles—have successfully survived numerous extinction events over many millions of years.

How dumb can they be?

Historically high numbers of species are rapidly becoming extinct as humans pollute, fragment, and destroy increasing amounts of habitat—both in the industrialized nations and in the impoverished countries of Central America, South America, and Central Africa that host the world's tropical rainforests.

Opposite: Reptile, mammal, and human footprints in the sand of the Sonoran Desert in the Coachella Valley of southern California.

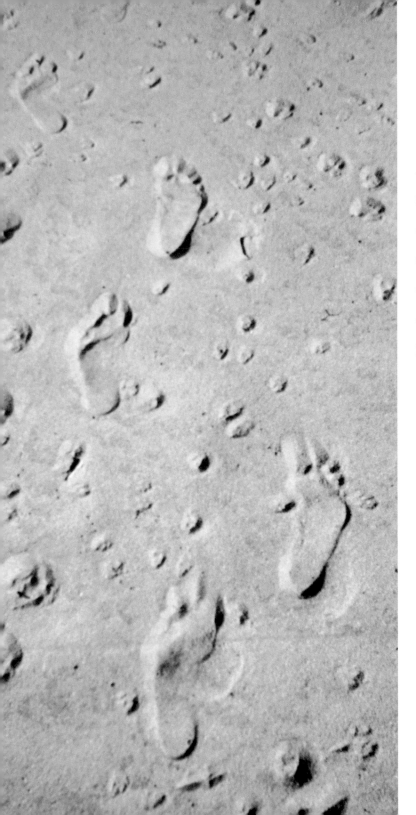

For we are strangers before
thee, and sojourners,
as were all our fathers:
our days on the earth
are as a shadow,
and there is none abiding.

DAVID, I CHRONICLES 29:15

Many scientists believe that a sixth major extinction event is now in progress. This would be the first extinction to be self-inflicted by life on Earth.

How dumb can we be?

The story of life's evolution proves that living creatures and their physical environment are inextricably linked. However, no matter how bad living conditions have become on Earth, a remnant of living creatures has always been left behind by death.

The remnant is our consolation prize—with or without our genes, it carries on.

Remarkably, several thousand years ago the ancient Hebrews understood the importance of the remnant *without* the benefit of analyzing fossils or genes.

Brave New World
. . . . .

For the fate of animals and the fate of humans is the same; as one dies, so dies the other. Who knows whether the human spirit goes upward and the spirit of animals goes downward to the earth?
ECCLESIASTES 3:19, 21 NRSV

As the result of their struggles to live under the covenant as the people of God, the Hebrews pioneered a whole new relationship not only with God, but also with Nature.

Belief in God as the supreme Creator led the Hebrews to see an underlying unity between the invisible divine presence and the physical world of Nature—a view that was unusual for early civilization.

While they probably didn't know about subatomic particles, molecules, elements, cells, and DNA, the Hebrews discerned through intuition and revelation what has now come to seem likely through tangible evidence: the inanimate and animate aspects of the cosmos are interconnected.

As a result, the Hebrews began to see Nature not as something to be worshiped as divine, but as something to be admired as the handiwork of God—the Creation. However, their relationships with both God and Nature changed gradually over several centuries.

Because of a geographic and genetic connection to the tropics, the Middle East has enjoyed a relatively high level of biodiversity and migration activity, which continues to this day outside the more developed and war-torn regions. For many millions of years, animals and humans have used an easily traveled route to the south of Palestine that links the Middle East and Africa.

Amid this abundant life and an agrarian lifestyle, Nature religions flourished in early Middle Eastern societies. Many adherents believed that there was a god in just about anything, and that these gods (baals) needed to be worshiped by humans and could be manipulated, given the right sacrifices.

These gods were not exactly higher powers.

Following the lead of Abraham, Isaac, Jacob, and Moses, the Hebrews began to turn away from these dominant beliefs and religious practices. But old habits die hard. The Hebrews had difficulty in reconciling Yahweh's omnipotence with the events of daily life. If Yahweh was the boss, why did bad things happen to them? When setbacks confronted them or they felt insecure, they often returned to other gods for help.

For example, when Moses lingered on Mount Sinai receiving the Ten Commandments, the people asked Aaron to fashion a god that would "go before them." Aaron complied with their request, as we see from Exodus 32:4 NRSV:

> *Even the stork in the sky*
> *knows her appointed seasons,*
> *and the dove, the swift and the thrush*
> *observe the time of their migration.*
> *But my people do not know*
> *the requirements of the Lord.*
> JEREMIAH 8:7

> He took the gold from them, formed it in a mold, and cast an image of a calf; and they said, "These are your gods, O Israel, who brought you up out of the land of Egypt."

Has the golden calf been reincarnated as cars, houses, work, and money?

Despite such lapses into idolatry, there was evidence of a changing relationship with Nature. In the Promised Land, the Hebrews became keen observers of the plants and animals around them, and they tried to understand God better by learning from Nature. Several books of the Old Testament, including Psalms,

Ecclesiastes, and Proverbs, include numerous references to wildlife, representing some of civilization's earliest Nature writing.

At least the Hebrews were well aware of their shortcomings in obeying God. Indeed, they had a special story that explained why God didn't just give up on humanity and trash the whole Earth to start life over with a clean slate.

The Remnant
. . . . .

But God sent me ahead of you to preserve for you a remnant on earth and to save your lives by a great deliverance.
JOSEPH TO HIS BROTHERS, GENESIS 45:7

In the story of Noah's ark, the Hebrews made sense of how humanity had survived God's wrath, and why rainbows appear in the sky. Genesis 6:12–14 tells how God became disgusted with humanity's corruption and decided to do away with the Earth:

> God saw how corrupt the earth had become, for all the people on earth had corrupted their ways. So God said to Noah, "I am going to put an end to all people, for the earth is filled with violence because of them. I am surely going to destroy both them and the earth. So make yourself an ark of cypress wood."

Since Noah was a righteous man, God told him how to build an ark and instructed him to take aboard his family and pairs of all living creatures and every kind of food. Noah obeyed God's instructions—well before it started raining.

Noah believed God without tangible evidence. Noah had faith.

Then, according to Genesis 7:23, a huge flood covered the Earth, with disastrous consequences:

> Every living thing on the face of the earth was wiped out; men and animals and the creatures that move along the ground and the birds of the air were wiped from the earth. Only Noah was left, and those with him in the ark.

Sounds like a major extinction event.

Eventually the waters receded, and God instructed Noah to bring everyone out of the ark to inhabit the Earth. God gave Noah permission to eat meat, and not just plants. However, this right to eat other creatures also carried responsibilities. In Genesis 9:5, God warned Noah that humans are expected to live righteously and look out for each other:

> And for your lifeblood I will surely demand an accounting. I will demand an accounting from every animal. And from each man, too, I will demand an accounting for the life of his fellow man.

Noah offered a pleasing sacrifice. Then, according to Genesis 9:12–15, God promised never again to allow such a severe flood on the Earth, despite human wickedness, and confirmed this promise with a sign:

> This is the sign of the covenant I am making between me and you and every living creature with you, a covenant for all generations to come: I have set my rainbow in the clouds, and it will be the sign of the covenant between me and the earth. . . . Never again will the waters become a flood to destroy all life.

In the story of Noah and throughout the Old Testament, God refused to let the Creation and humanity die out because God had other plans for them. A remnant was always left behind after every disaster—as in the evolution of life on Earth.

Left behind—for what?

Although the Hebrews understood that God had made the Creation for a reason, the divine purpose for it was not quite clear to them. If God had created everything and saw that it was good, why was there so much unfairness, suffering, and death on Earth? If God had made humans in the divine image, why were they inclined toward evil and wrongdoing?

Hate evil, love good;
maintain justice in the courts.
Perhaps the Lord God Almighty
will have mercy on the remnant of Joseph.
Amos 5:15

What was God thinking? Better yet, what is God thinking?

Despite these questions, the Hebrews knew that God was up to something. They knew that, no matter what, God would not give up on the Creation and humanity, as Isaiah 6:11–13 confirms:

Whenever the rainbow appears in the clouds, I will see it and remember the everlasting covenant between God and all living creatures of every kind on the earth.

God to Noah, Genesis 9:16

And though a tenth remains in the land, it will again be laid waste.
But as the terebinth and oak leave stumps when they are cut down,
so the holy seed will be the stump in the land.

Soultrinos are the holy seed that always overcomes the dark energy and bears fruit.

Although the Hebrews didn't know that God has been working on this Creation project for almost fourteen billion years, they knew that God is supremely patient and relentless in pursuing the divine purpose.

God wants something from the Creation—and is determined to get it.

Nothing stops God—not dark energy, asteroids, climate change, mass extinctions, or humans.

Whatever God is up to, the Hebrews understood that humanity and Nature are in the same ark: one God, one Creation, one purpose, and one destiny.

What is the kingdom of God like? . . . It is like a mustard seed, which a man took and planted in his garden. It grew and became a tree, and the birds of the air perched in its branches. JESUS, LUKE 13:18–19	The Holy Seed . . . . .

As did his Hebrew ancestors, Jesus admired and respected the Creation as a great teacher on spiritual matters. However, he focused more intently on the presence of evil in the Creation and on God's ultimate purpose for the Creation.

Although the Old Testament contains references to evil, evil is not clearly depicted as the work of a being or a force. Nevertheless, Jesus' teachings are unequivocal on this issue. In all four gospels, he made it clear that there is something in the Creation that is not willing to collaborate with God's will. He referred to this presence as Satan, Beelzebub, the devil, and evil.

The devil is the spiritual equivalent of dark energy—the universe's self-destructive streak.

Opposite: A rainbow rises behind Black Mountain after an unusual morning storm in early October.

Like Isaiah and the other prophets, Jesus repeatedly used seeds and plants as metaphors in his teachings.

Visible seeds contain the invisible divine potential of life—the soultrinos.

Generally, seeds that are properly planted and nourished sprout into plants and bear fruit. However, the forces of Nature can disrupt this process and keep a seed from fulfilling its potential. In the parable of the sower from Luke 8:5–8, Jesus taught that God is like a farmer who generously sowed seed with mixed results:

> A farmer went out to sow his seed. As he was scattering the seed, some fell along the path; it was trampled on, and the birds of the air ate it up. Some fell on rock, and when it came up, the plants withered because they had no moisture. Other seed fell among thorns, which grew up with it and choked the plants. Still other seed fell on good soil. It came up and yielded a crop, a hundred times more than was sown.

When his disciples asked him to explain this parable, Jesus' answer suggested that this beloved Creation is not the full reflection of God's divine presence. There's some spiritual interference, as Jesus explained in Luke 8:11–15:

> This is the meaning of the parable: The seed is the word of God. Those along the path are the ones who hear, and then the devil comes and takes away the word from their hearts, so that they may not believe and be saved. Those on the rock are the ones who receive the word with joy when they hear it, but they have no root. They believe for a while, but in the time of testing they fall away. The seed that fell among thorns stands for those who hear, but as they go on their way they are choked by life's worries, riches and pleasures, and they do not mature. But the seed on good soil stands for those with a noble and good heart, who hear the word, retain it, and by persevering produce a crop.

Through his explanation of this parable, Jesus affirmed that the physical universe is not aligned with God's will. God has always wanted the Creation to have abundance, not shortage; growth, not diminishment; purpose, not hopelessness; and life, not death. However, a force called "the devil" (or Satan) has been a spoiler, with the power to rebel against God's will—just like we do.

Opposite: Continental Mountain watches over a blooming hedgehog cactus.

And why do you worry about clothes? See how the lilies of the field grow. They do not labor or spin. Yet I tell you that even Solomon in all his splendor was not dressed like one of these.

Jesus,
Matthew 6:28–29

How did Satan come to be in the Creation? The only clue Jesus left behind is this passage from Luke 10:18 NRSV:

I watched Satan fall from heaven like a flash of lightning.

What was Jesus' relationship with this "bad seed" in the Creation? It was not what we might expect.

Often, Jesus showed a cool indifference toward Satan—as if Satan were an uncaring, impersonal presence in contrast to God's intensely caring, personal presence. With God, it's personal and friendly. With Satan, it's anonymous and hostile.

Satan is the cruel, indifferent streak in Nature—and in us.

At times, Jesus seemed to treat Satan like a naughty younger sibling. He reprimanded and disciplined Satan, and even ordered Satan around. Once when Jesus predicted his own death, his disciple Peter responded in a way that provoked an intriguing response from Jesus, as Matthew 16:22–23 NRSV reveals:

And Peter took him aside and began to rebuke him, saying, "God forbid it, Lord! This must never happen to you." But he turned and said to Peter, "Get behind me, Satan! You are a stumbling block to me; for you are setting your mind not on divine things but on human things."

We attract Satan's lightning with the spiritual dead wood of egotism, fear, and greed.

Surprisingly, Jesus even seemed to appreciate that Satan had a constructive role to play in the Creation. He knew that Satan had a way of influencing people from the inside out, and played an active role in tempting people, as he warned Peter in Luke 22:31–32 NRSV:

Simon, Simon, listen! Satan has demanded to sift all of you like wheat, but I have prayed for you that your own faith may not fail; and you, when once you have turned back, strengthen your brothers.

Yet Jesus didn't talk about hurting, killing, or destroying Satan, as if Satan's fate were up to God and not to him or us. Rather, he taught that Satan is a spiritual enemy, to be overcome with spiritual power. To overpower Satan, humans must be as gentle and persistent as plants are in fulfilling their potential.

God created a universe that would help Satan become collaborative.

To become aligned with God's will and overcome Satan, in John 12:24 Jesus urged people to allow selfishness to die and to serve the interests of others:

> I tell you the truth, unless a kernel of wheat falls to the ground and dies, it remains only a single seed. But if it dies, it produces many seeds.

In order to realize God's will, we need to make some choices that run contrary to the tendencies of Nature. The rest of the Creation is bound by the natural principles and instincts that govern the physical world, and doesn't have the spiritual freedom in relationships that we do. God wants us to use this freedom to bear good spiritual fruit in our thoughts, speech, and behavior, as Jesus suggested in Luke 6:44–45:

> People do not pick figs from thornbushes, or grapes from briers. The good man brings good things out of the good stored up in his heart, and the evil man brings evil things out of the evil stored up in his heart. For out of the overflow of his heart his mouth speaks.

Even though Satan is a formidable opponent, Jesus repeatedly assured us that God is more powerful than Satan, and that God is always there to help us in our struggles with Satan. Once we choose to bear good spiritual fruit, God helps us to bear even more, as Jesus indicated in John 15:1–2:

> I am the true vine, and my Father is the gardener. He cuts off every branch in me that bears no fruit, while every branch that does bear fruit he prunes so that it will be even more fruitful.

Above everything else, Jesus taught us to put our relationships with the divine family (God, the Creation, others, and self) ahead of our material needs, as Luke 12:29–31 affirms:

> And do not set your heart on what you will eat or drink; do not worry about it. For the pagan world runs after all such things, and your Father knows that you need them. But seek his kingdom, and these things will be given to you as well.

We need to show Satan he can't hide from God in our hearts.

Despite the interference of Satan, Jesus' teachings made it clear that God wants us to reap the kingdom's spiritual harvest of love, forgiveness, righteousness, and peace in this world. If we won't, God will find someone who will, as Jesus indicated in Matthew 21:43:

> Therefore I tell you that the kingdom of God will be taken away from you and given to a people who will produce its fruit.

No other member of the Creation has the spiritual freedom to help gather the kingdom's harvest. We are the only ones who can prepare the way for what Jesus called "the renewal of all things" in Matthew 19:28.

The renewal of all things—when soultrinos make the universe a friendly place.

It's up to us. It's our move. The universe cannot be a friendly place on its own. It's our job to help make it that way—all other jobs are filled here on Earth.

How long will it take? How long will God wait?

Together for Life
. . . . .

The love of life, at any and every level of development, is the religious impulse.

WILLIAM JAMES, *The Varieties of Religious Experience*

Based on scientific evidence, the story of life's evolution offers proof of what the world's spiritual leaders and mystics have been telling humanity for thousands of years: all of Nature, both animate and inanimate, is hewn from the same rock and quarry. It all exists within one vast, interconnected web.

A chemical, electromagnetic, genetic web connecting God, Nature, and us.

In the thirteenth century, the great Christian mystic Meister Eckhart preached in the Rhine Valley of Germany that all creatures are the thoughts of God.

The most famous Christian mystic, Saint Francis of Assisi, boldly proclaimed the brotherhood of humanity and the whole Creation from his vantage point in thirteenth-century Italy. Francis was renowned for his dynamic sermons and special relationship with animals—he even preached to *them* to be thankful to God!

Lady Julian of Norwich, another prominent Christian mystic who lived in fourteenth-century England, described a vision from God in which she saw a tiny round ball in her hand and wondered what it was:

The answer came: "This is all that is made." I felt it was so small that it could easily fade to nothing; but again I was told, "This lasts and will go on lasting forever because God loves it. And so it is with every being that God loves." I saw three properties about this tiny object: First, God has made it; second, God loves it. And third, God keeps it.

A grapefruit of matter and a hazelnut of soultrinos underwrote the universe.

Lady Julian's vision confirmed that the Creation has an enduring spiritual nature despite its fragile physical nature, and that all aspects of the Creation—animate and inanimate—are precious to God.

> *To cooperate in the highest as well as the lowest sense, means to get our living together.*
> HENRY DAVID THOREAU, *Walden*

If we love God, we must love what God has created, and collaborate with the Creation. There's no life to waste here on Earth. Only God knows the Creation from the inside out—how it works and the purpose of every species and every creature.

To mess with the environment is to mess with life, and to mess with life is to mess with God.

Everything in the Creation has an important lesson to teach us about the web of life and the thoughts of God—and how we fit into both. In order to survive, we must identify, study, and cooperate with species rather than annihilate them.

Living creatures deserve respect just for showing up.

Brother Sun and the other stars, Sister Moon, Mother Earth, and all her children are our companions in the ark of physical existence—but no one has been equipped for existence quite as we have.

Finally, we are beginning to understand just how exquisite our equipment truly is—and what we are supposed to do with it.

· · · · ·

> *Who goes there? Hankering, gross, mystical, nude;*
> *How is it I extract strength from the beef I eat?*
> *What is a man anyhow? what am I? what are you?*
> WALT WHITMAN, *"Song of Myself"*

SONORAN SUMMER VESPERS

Brother Sun calls goodnight
as he turns out the light.
Thanks be to God.

The mountains smile and wink
as they watch him sink.
Thanks be to God.

The Desert heaves a sigh
as she says goodbye.
Thanks be to God.

Quail bathe in the dust
and settle in with a fuss.
Thanks be to God.

Bunnies jump and zip
after one last sip.
Thanks be to God.

Hummers twitter and hover
as they take cover.
Thanks be to God.

Nighthawks swoop and thrill
with an eerie trill.
Thanks be to God.

Thrashers call whit-wheet
from their cholla seat.
Thanks be to God.

Bats swoop and dart
with fits and starts.
Thanks be to God.

Javelinas woof and snort
as they yonder cavort.
Thanks be to God.

Packrats chew and chomp
while their babies romp.
Thanks be to God.

Snakes slither around
as they prowl the ground.
Thanks be to God.

Bugs start to sing
as they spread their wings.
Thanks be to God.

Toads come on out
and start jumping about.
Thanks be to God.

Owls glide and hoot
while they hunt for loot.
Thanks be to God.

Sister Moon cries hello
to her family below.
Thanks be to God.

People close the door
and doze off with a snore.
Thanks be to God.

Even the Prince of Light
is in love with the night.
Thanks be to God.

Above: Clouds bring spectacular sunsets to the Sonoran Desert.

FOUR

Self

The word is very near to you; it is in your mouth and in your heart for you to observe.
MOSES, DEUTERONOMY 30:14

You will know the truth, and the truth will make you free.
JESUS, JOHN 8:32

I do not understand my own actions. For I do not do what I want, but I do the very thing I hate. . . . I can will what is right, but I cannot do it.
PAUL, ROMANS 7:15–18

The prime characteristic of cosmic consciousness is. . .a consciousness of the life and order of the universe. Our descendants will sooner or later reach cosmic consciousness, just as long ago, our ancestors passed from simple to self consciousness.
RICHARD MAURICE BUCKE, *Cosmic Consciousness*

Opposite: A male rufous-backed hummingbird
pauses briefly, revealing his iridescent crimson gorget.

The invasion started on July 12 this year, right around the time that it usually starts.

Every year, a thundering herd sweeps down and assails the entire Salt River Valley, intimidating the locals with reddish, warlike colors, loud noise, and naked aggression.

Eventually the locals retool their nerves, replacing flesh and blood with steel to endure the frequent battles over food and turf that become part of daily life.

Around mid-September, as suddenly and unpredictably as they arrived, the invaders depart to head south for the winter.

These are the real snowbirds: the feisty Allen's and rufous hummingbirds, who merely pass through our area to summer as far north as Canada and to winter in Mexico. They don't nest here; they just eat a few meals, pick a few fights, and move on.

Every spring they pillage and plunder their way north. Then they head back down south as autumn approaches, often via a different route. Unlike the human version of snowbirds, they travel with no baggage, just memories and bravado.

I am hummer, hear me whirr.
Tropical forests are my home.
Bright flowers are my chef.
Strong winds are my chariot.
Treetops are for trysts.
Watch me fly if you can,
Poor land-bound stumbler.
I am hummerrrrrrrrrrrrrrrrr!

Between the steering winds of the atmosphere and the Earth's magnetic field, these migratory hummers navigate exceptionally well, and often stop in the same spots from year to year. Yet even with such help, their journeys can be exhausting.

One July afternoon, I observed a male hummer atop a tall dried bouquet in a protected corner of our back porch. The poor little fellow was trembling and shuddering violently, as if hyperventilating. His appearance coincided with a dry, windy low-pressure system sweeping through our area, so he had probably just finished a leg of his migration. I imagine he was fiercely hungry once he recovered from his effort.

Around here, the spring babies of the year-round resident Anna's and Costa's hummingbirds have to grow up fast, because by the time they are two months old they need to be ready for war.

The Hummer Wars. Coming this summer to a feeder near you.

Now *this* is reality programming worth watching!

> *There can be no very black melancholy to him who lives in the midst of Nature and has his senses still.*
> HENRY DAVID THOREAU, *Walden*

The Lonely Crowd
. . . . .

There's something about hummers.

While hummers are native to the Americas, only a handful of states in the United States have year-round hummer populations. The hummer is most at home in the tropics, where its ancestors coevolved with flowering plants over the past hundred million years.

A long, narrow tongue that extends well beyond its beak is the hummer's secret weapon for getting to the sweet nectar of flowers. Hummers favor flowers of orange, red, and purple shades, with a trumpet shape that makes them perfectly suited to the hummer's tongue.

As one of the smallest warm-blooded vertebrates and one of the smartest birds, the hummer is a diminutive marvel of Nature.

However, there's a quiet intelligence and great tenacity behind all that smallness, as I learned one spring when a female Costa's hummingbird took me under her wing and taught me something about hummers.

She appeared one warm, sunny afternoon in our version of spring (late February), carefully building a nest in a nearby tree. Back and forth she repeatedly flew with lichen and plant scraps, sounding like a hushed helicopter. She gently visited all the spiderwebs in the yard, taking a little from each rather than ruining any one web. She used the spider silk to reinforce her nest, just two inches in diameter.

Daily she would make her rounds, periodically feasting on the same plants. She would go to each little flower, sticking her long, narrow tongue deep down to lick some nectar. Her frequent visits let the plants know that their efforts were appreciated, so in effect she was priming the nectar pump. She favored the blooms of native agave, chuparosa, ocotillo, and penstemon, as well as a few nonnative sages like Texas sage and autumn sage.

One impulse from a vernal wood
May teach you more of man
Of moral evil and of good
Than all the sages can.
WILLIAM WORDSWORTH

For many days in mid- to late March, she spent hours on the nest and allowed me to observe from just a few feet away, probably tolerating me as a deterrent to predators.

What a spectacle—this bird, weighing but three-tenths of an ounce, sitting on a miniature nest, determined to hatch and fledge even tinier babies, despite the cold, windy spells or sudden heat waves that so often arise in early spring.

Yet how very proud she appeared, sitting on that petite nest. Her head and beak pointed slightly upward, and her eyes shone with divine vitality, as if the Creator himself had fathered her babies.

That spring a freakish cold snap brought several snowfalls in early April. Most people remember the season because so many national golf tournaments were canceled. But the outcome was far worse for this nesting hummer, whom I had named Little Mama.

All of Little Mama's efforts on the nest were for naught. Her babies froze to death.

Little Mama did not seem overly distraught about the tragedy. She immediately busied herself building a new nest in the same tree, just a few feet from the old one. *No time lost to grief or depression. She just kept trying.*

She must have quickly seduced one of the handsome Costa's males—perhaps the one I called Boy Gorgeous, with his stunning, iridescent violet gorget. Maybe

she roused him early one morning from the tree out front in which he sleeps, asking to see some of his sky dives—his proof that he's got the right stuff.

Soon enough there were two very tiny heads popping out of the nest, each one pointed slightly upward, just like Little Mama's when she had been hatching the eggs. Their eyes beamed with that same divine vitality, as if they knew the fate of their unborn siblings and were happy to be alive.

Repeatedly Little Mama left the nest and returned with food, each time met by babies trying to outsqueal each other: "I'm hungrier." "No, *I'm* hungrier!"

For at least two weeks, poor Little Mama had to do this all by herself. The male

Above: This female Anna's hummingbird can maneuver in flight much like a helicopter, which is especially helpful in navigating the tall blooms of an agave.

hummer's contribution to the child-rearing process is to depart from the nesting territory so he doesn't compete with the mother and babies for food.

One morning in early May, Little Mama perched about a foot above the nest for minutes at a time—highly unusual behavior. She was probably urging her babies to fly out of the nest, because late that afternoon the nest was empty. Just like that, the tiny nestlings became fledglings.

By dusk that evening the fledglings were right back in the same tree near the nest, patiently waiting for night to fall.

Of course they came back to that tree. Where else? That was home—for now.

For several days the fledglings continued to beg Little Mama for food with a sweetly pathetic yet dignified sound. She kept feeding them, fairly and patiently.

The juveniles were fun to have around, amusing in their aerial acrobatics as they learned to fly, hover, and compete with one another.

Not long after the fledging, one day Little Mama happened by as her favorite plant, an autumn sage with magenta blossoms, was getting a spray. She started to fly away, but then turned back. She zigzagged back and forth in the spray for a minute or so, enjoying the shower that serendipity had brought her way.

> *Dance, hummingbird, dance*
> *back and forth in the cooling mist.*
> *Your babies have flown*
> *and once again*
> *you're all alone.*
> *So dance, hummingbird, dance.*
> *Dance for the joy*
> *of being alive*
> *on a warm spring morn in the Desert.*

Little Mama took off a couple of weeks later after teaching her fledglings how to find nectar, hawk insects, and defend their territory.

And it's a good thing she taught them well, because once July rolled around, the war began. Again.

In defending a food source, hummers display a heartless ferocity that seems totally incongruent with their size and intelligence. They engage in violent body checking and high-speed pursuit to protect their sips of nectar.

They can be lonely, aggressive little control freaks, even in a crowd of hummers.

These tendencies I've witnessed in Little Mama and other hummers have led me to wonder about where evolution has been and where it is headed.

Is this the best result that 100 million years of avian evolution has been able to deliver—an exquisite, exceptionally smart creature that leads such a solitary, combative existence?

Why didn't evolution make hummers kinder?

How did humans evolve from primates in only five million years, an evolutionary blink of the eye, while other creatures like the scorpion have stayed virtually unchanged for four hundred million years?

What makes us similar to other animals—and what makes us different?

Is our species subject to the same forces of self-destruction and collaboration as the rest of Nature?

Is evolution finished with our species—or are we a work in progress?

Where is evolution trying to take all of us?

Is it someplace we want to go?

Whether we like it or not, evolution tells a story that we need to understand: the story of us. *All* of us.

The story that will set us free.

Man with all his noble qualities, with sympathy which feels for the most debased . . . with all these exalted powers man still bears in his bodily frame the indelible stamp of his lowly origin. CHARLES DARWIN, *The Descent of Man*	*Out of Africa* · · · · ·

Since Charles Darwin published his seminal work on evolution, *The Origin of Species,* in 1862, evolution has matured from a preposterous theory to the most likely scenario of how we all got here.

For us humans, there's good news and there's bad news.

The good news is that we evolved from the most intelligent, sociable group of animals that has ever lived on the Earth: primates. This is the order of mammals that includes gorillas, orangutans, chimpanzees, and humans.

The bad news is that it wasn't that long ago. The first hominids (human ancestors) appeared about five million years ago, so we have evolved at the evolutionary equivalent of the speed of light. However, as a species, we still need some work—we're not quite done evolving.

Fortunately, our evolutionary story sheds some light on what it means to be human—how we're similar to other animals, how we're different, and where we're headed.

Why is it so difficult to understand what it means to be a human?

Despite the current sketchy understanding of the human genome, it is clear that our genes do not make us unique. Strikingly different animals have many common genes. For example, the human genome is about 98 percent similar to that of the chimpanzee.

In part, this extensive similarity is linked to Nature's fondness for efficiency—she hates to recreate the wheel. Once Nature perfects something like a heart or a lung in a land animal, she likes to reuse the same genetic model across many different species. In addition, Nature prefers to repurpose old genes rather than abandon them when their usefulness is diminished.

Hurrah for positive science! Long live exact demonstration! . . .
This is the geologist, this works with a scalpel, and this is a mathematician.
Gentleman, to you the first honors always!
Your facts are useful, and yet they are not my dwelling,
I but enter by them to an area of my dwelling.
WALT WHITMAN, *"Song of Myself"*

Recently it has become clear that the degree to which a gene is switched on (expressed) plays a major role in genetic functions. Gene expression can be highly influenced by the environment and experience, in a way that is still not well understood.

Opposite: Although mammals are difficult to observe in the Sonoran Desert, they can occasionally be seen at rest, like this young javelina.

I think I could turn and live with animals, they are so placid and self-contained,

I stand and look at them long and long....

So they show their relations to me and I accept them,

They bring me tokens of myself, they evince them plainly in their possession.

I wonder where they get those tokens,

Did I pass that way huge times ago and negligently drop them?

WALT WHITMAN, *"Song of Myself"*

Genes, experiences, and thoughts shape our behavior.

If it's not our genes, then what is it that makes us so different from other animals?

For starters, we are the only living creatures on Earth that have ever stood up straight and walked upright. We take walking upright for granted, yet it is unique in Nature.

Like most primates, our ancestors depended on large trees for food. About five million years ago, the usual suspects of geological activity and climate change caused trees to disappear in East Africa. Hungry primates had to travel farther to find food.

In response to this crisis, the earliest hominids began to stand upright, vertically aligning the Earth's gravity, feet, head, and sun for the first time in evolutionary history. This posture allowed greater mobility and social interaction. Suddenly these social animals could more easily look straight into one another's eyes.

Could a greater miracle take place than for us to look through each other's eyes for an instant?
HENRY DAVID THOREAU, *Walden*

This new posture greatly enhanced cognitive stimulation, triggering a phenomenal growth in the brain capacity of hominids that was also unique in evolutionary terms. Today, our brains are about four times the size of those of the earliest hominids.

Gravity, sunshine, and eye contact let the soultrinos in and allow the brain to grow.

One of the main benefits of this growing brainpower has been a knack for tools and innovation—another significant difference between us and other living creatures. About two million years ago, the earliest members of our genus *Homo*, *Homo habilis*, used their remarkable brainpower to craft new and improved tools for acquiring food.

However, these early innovators never advanced much in their toolmaking techniques over the next million years, and might have become extinct as a result.

We need to innovate to survive. Technology isn't the problem—our use of it is.

Furthermore, we appear to be very different from other animals in that we have no living relatives. Exactly why this is the case is still a mystery.

Forty thousand years ago, members of our species, the Cro-Magnons, had arrived in ice age Europe and were coexisting with our last living relatives, the Neanderthals. Over the next ten thousand years, the harsh climatic conditions peaked as glaciers crept south and long winters endured. During this period, our ice-age-savvy Neanderthal cousins became extinct and our Cro-Magnon ancestors blossomed, painting pictures on cave walls and playing music.

Why did our species prevail, and why did the Neanderthals fail? The answer does not appear to be violence between the two species, since there is no evidence of warfare or widespread fighting.

Over many winters, both Neanderthals and humans probably had to stay in caves for long periods. Even with all our modern diversions, we get cabin fever under such conditions—imagine the "cave fever" they must have experienced.

Cave rage—the hominid ancestor of road rage.

During those long winters, as boredom, hunger, and lust continually tempted the Neanderthals and Cro-Magnons in their separate caves, how did each respond?

Did the Neanderthals' fertility dry up owing to the stress of unrelenting social tension? Did our Cro-Magnon ancestors figure out that laughing, music, art, singing, dancing, and romance were more entertaining than violence? Did Cro-Magnon men use intimacy and tenderness to seduce the Neanderthal women away from their irascible mates?

Intimate physical and spiritual expressions of love are at the root of our humanity.

Anatomy might have helped seal our cousins' fate. The Neanderthals' strong, bulky frame was advantageous for hunting and self-defense but not for migration. Our hapless cousins might have been unable to migrate as the ice and snow closed in and the food disappeared.

Did they become hopeless and give up, victims of their soul-ache?

Somehow, we out-smiled, out-laughed, out-loved, out-walked, or out-hoped the Neanderthals.

Regardless of what happened to our Neanderthal relatives, our unique evolu-

What behaved well in the past or behaves well to-day is not such a wonder,
The wonder is always and always how there can be a mean man or an infidel.
WALT WHITMAN, *"Song of Myself"*

tionary story implies that what makes us most different from other animals is all in our heads.

The Inner Child
· · · · ·

Every child begins the world again, to some extent, and loves to stay outdoors, even in wet and cold.

HENRY DAVID THOREAU, *Walden*

A human head really should come with an owner's manual, but unfortunately it does not. Despite decades of research, how the amazing contents of our head—the hardware called the brain and the software called the mind—really work is still a mystery.

Based on what is known, everyone with a brain should be aware of several important realities about our psychic lay of the land.

Nature has whipped up much of our cerebral hardware from genetic leftovers. This should not surprise us, since it is very clear that Nature prefers to reuse existing genetic structures. Much of what our brain does daily is similar to what the brains of other animals do daily, such as manage bodily functions and movements and generate responses to external events.

As a result, Nature has cobbled together a somewhat unwieldy brain for us from a combination of the old and the new. The three major components of our brain are the reptilian brain (the oldest area, similar to the brain of a modern reptile); the mammalian brain (an old area, similar to the brain of a nonhuman modern mammal), and the human brain (a very young area also called the cortex, unique to *Homo sapiens*).

What are the practical implications of this curious arrangement of gray matter? To understand what is really going on in our heads, we must look at both our cerebral hardware and software (the mental experiences that we call the mind).

Referring to "the mind" is somewhat misleading, because we actually have two minds: the unconscious mind and the conscious mind. Remarkably, we switch between them continually throughout the day, depending on what we are thinking or doing, and what is going on around us.

From the bottom and back of the brain, the oldest areas—the reptilian and mammalian brains—run the basic functions of both physical and psychic life, and generate the unconscious mind. Interestingly, the ancient reptilian brain controls the toggle switch that determines who's in charge at any given time—the unconscious or conscious mind.

We are conscious of an animal in us, which awakens in proportion as our higher nature slumbers. It is reptile and sensual. . . . Possibly we may withdraw from it, but never change its nature.

HENRY DAVID THOREAU, *Walden*

Our inner reptile tends to run our psychic life!

Most of us think of the unconscious mind as a stranger, that remote presence that brings us bizarre dreams while we are sleeping. While the unconscious mind does indeed bring us dreams, it is no stranger—it is the dominant force in our daily psychic life.

The unconscious mind is the window of the soul.

Our unconscious mind can be understood easily from the world around us. Any young child, cat, or dog shows us that the unconscious mind continually generates responses to the environment, including instincts, urges, appetites, and emotions. They also show us that the unconscious mind enjoys the experiential world of the here and now, particularly in Nature.

If the unconscious mind connects us to Nature and God, then babies are spiritual geniuses.

I have always been regretting that I was not as wise as the day I was born.

HENRY DAVID THOREAU, *Walden*

The unconscious mind is the hard-working operating system of daily psychic life. So what is left for the conscious mind to do?

Plenty.

Like walking upright, we tend to take self-consciousness (let's just call it consciousness) for granted. Yet apparently no other creature has ever experienced this mental state, which allows us to observe what's going on around us as well as what's going on within us. From the top of the brain, the cortex creates consciousness through four lobes, each with special tasks:

Occipital (back): vision

Parietal (back-center): movement, spatial awareness, calculation

Temporal (front-center): sound, music, speech, memory

Frontal (front): abstract and symbolic thought, feelings, attention, willfulness

The oldest parts of the cortex are in the back (occipital and parietal lobes), while the most recently evolved parts are in the front (temporal and frontal lobes). The frontal lobe is the executive area of the conscious mind, and it runs the show.

Most of us have a tendency to use one or two of these lobes more heavily than the others, and this imbalance has a major influence on personality. Not coincidentally, personality classification schemes from Plato to Jung to Myers-Briggs (and even *The Wizard of Oz*) have been based on four major categories.

On each side of the human brain, these lobes have somewhat different functions, so that popularly they are referred to as the "left brain" and the "right brain." Simplistically, the left brain tends to focus on language, details, and intellectual activity, and the right brain tends to focus on patterns, intuition, and emotional activity.

As I see my soul reflected in Nature,
As I see through a mist, One with
inexpressible completeness, sanity, beauty,
See the bent head and arms folded
over the breast, the Female I see.
WALT WHITMAN,
"I Sing the Body Electric"

The left and right brains share information through a band of nerves called the corpus callosum, which happens to be considerably thicker in women than in men.

Women are better wired for consciousness.

What special powers does consciousness give us? Consciousness allows us to reflect so that we can understand why we think, feel, and act the way we do—and to change how we think, feel, and act.

To be human is to understand and control one's own mind.

Do feelings come from the conscious mind—or from the unconscious mind?

Opposite: Just as this ocotillo and saguaro prosper close together, the unconscious mind blossoms in natural settings.

That's a trick question. There is a huge difference between emotions, which are generated by the unconscious mind, and feelings, which are the product of the conscious mind.

All mammals share certain emotions, such as fear, greed, anger, rivalry, sadness, disgust, surprise, contempt, and contentment. Just check in with the nearest dog, cat, or three-year-old to confirm that fact. However, only adults can experience a wide range of feelings, including love, compassion, humility, gratitude, kindness, hopefulness, fulfillment, serenity, faith, and a zest for life. Just check in with the nearest mature human to confirm that fact.

Emotions are pan-mammalian; feelings are human.

Emotions are a natural reaction to external events, conditioned by almost three hundred million years of mammalian evolutionary experience. In humans, the frontal lobe turns the impersonal emotional and instinctual responses of the unconscious mind into personal feelings from the heart. Frontal lobe afflictions— such as addiction, depression, anxiety, attention deficit disorder, and schizophrenia—interfere with the ability to convert emotions into feelings.

Another special power that consciousness gives us is symbolic thought. This thought process allows us to connect a visible, perceptible object with an invisible thought or feeling. This capacity underlies our ability to communicate with images, words, numbers, and music.

To be human is to connect the seen with the unseen.

The conscious mind also has the special power to construct its own version of reality. From there, it can imagine what is going on in other people's minds, as well as build a reality that is more to its liking—and easier to control—than the one outside.

Nature abhors a vacuum—but the conscious mind loves one.

In contrast to the unconscious mind's penchant for the here and now, the conscious mind likes to spend time in its own future-oriented world, a world built from ambitions, fantasies, activities, goals, projects, deadlines, achievements, and delusions.

The adult conscious mind likes to play God—so it tries to shut God out.

Like a newly installed but highly complex computer program, the conscious mind performs some amazing feats, but it also has a tendency to crash frequently. What is it that makes the conscious mind freeze up and crash?

The answer appears to be much the same as for software: compatibility problems. Just as operating systems and application software may encounter conflicts and disruptions when they try to work together, the unconscious and conscious minds can have relationship issues.

Our inner child is in there, playing and fighting with our inner reptile and inner mammal.

The renowned Swiss psychologist Carl Gustav Jung was dedicated to understanding the unconscious mind's role in psychic life and human behavior. He found that the unconscious mind tries to alert the conscious mind to both physical threats (for example, disease or nutritional deficits) as well as mental threats (for example, ignorance, mistakes, or delusions). However, the conscious mind has a tendency to selfishly disregard unconscious messages.

The incessant strain and anxiety of some is a well-nigh incurable form of disease. We are made to exaggerate the importance of what work we do; and yet how much is not done by us!
HENRY DAVID THOREAU, *Walden*

The conscious mind needs to learn how to say, "I'm OK, you're OK" to the unconscious mind.

Jung believed that the unconscious mind accesses information through the "collective unconscious," a vast unseen reservoir of cumulative human knowledge and experience. He considered the unconscious mind to be more helpful than harmful—unless its contents are ignored or repressed. Then the unconscious mind tries to get attention through slips of the tongue, difficulty in remembering important things, pain, illness, or provoking accidents (for example, cutting one's finger with a knife).

A sweet spot in the unconscious mind attracts the cosmic forces of collaboration and self-destruction.

Relationship tension between the unconscious and conscious minds can make consciousness crash and disassociate intention and behavior, as described by Paul

I rejoice that there are owls. Let them do the idiotic and maniacal hooting for men. . . . They represent the stark twilight and unsatisfied thoughts which all have.

HENRY DAVID THOREAU, *Walden*

in one of the opening quotes for this chapter. Such mental conflict is often at the root of anxiety, unhappiness, violence, and other negative experiences.

The human brain is still evolving, as Nature tries to smooth out the glitches in our cerebral network. And we shouldn't feel so bad about where things stand—it took birds ten million years to figure out how to fly right.

If we can avoid self-destruction long enough, some day our species will naturally enjoy a much more stable, happy, peaceful version of consciousness.

The purpose of the human brain is to reconcile self-destruction and collaboration.

Fortunately, that is exactly what the Bible is all about: how to become more conscious and happy, and how to prepare for what lies ahead.

Does evolution want us to form a collective conscious?

So God created humankind in his image, in the image of God he created them; male and female he created them. GENESIS 1:27	**The Forbidden Fruit**

While the ancient Hebrews might not have known the difference between the mammalian brain and the cortex, they clearly understood human nature all too well. They understood that the human condition is defined by an inner conflict between what someone wants to do (desire) and what someone ought to do (duty).

Desire and duty—the spiritual guardrails for staying on the path of right relationship.

As the Hebrews tried to understand how humans were different from other creatures, they discerned that humans were made in the image of God. This special relationship between humans and God allowed them to share a common language: the word of God, or the divine wisdom of God.

This language—the word of God—is accessible to the human mind, as indicated in Moses' words at the beginning of this chapter. Unlike other creatures,

Opposite: A great horned owl nestling looks down from a secure spot in the arms of a mature saguaro.

humans need the spiritual sustenance of God's wisdom as much as they need physical nourishment.

Yet despite this bond with the divine, the Hebrews realized that humans have an innate tendency to do what is morally wrong: to miss the mark, or sin, through a conscious, willful choice of what one desires over what one knows to be right.

Sin—to miss the mark of being human by choosing to follow one's inner reptile or mammal.

The Hebrews were intrigued by the question "Why do we do what we do?" The story of "the fall" of Adam and his mate Eve (found in Genesis 3:1–19) was their inspired way of making sense of the human condition as they experienced it.

This story is of great value to us today, not in explaining the details of humanity's physical evolution but in understanding the development of human consciousness and spirituality.

Given the arid setting in which the Hebrews lived, it is understandable that they pictured the original paradise as a lush garden—perhaps similar to the subtropical setting in which humans first evolved.

As Genesis tells the story, God set the first human up in a pretty good situation. God made a deal: the human would take care of the bountiful Garden of Eden and in return could eat anything in it—except the fruit of a forbidden tree. God gave freedom, and asked for responsibility in return.

God wants to have a give-and-take relationship with humans—and to be friends.

Since the human was lonely, God created a partner. The first human had no gender until the partner was created—no maleness existed without femaleness. Neither human had a name at this point.

One day, a serpent tempted the woman to eat the forbidden fruit. He was clever in his approach, even getting her to recite the "deal" that she and her husband had with God, as Genesis 3:1–5 relates:

> Now the serpent was more crafty than any of the wild animals the Lord God had made. He said to the woman, "Did God really say, 'You must not eat from any tree in the garden'"?
>
> The woman said to the serpent, "We may eat fruit from the trees in the garden,

but God did say, 'You must not eat fruit from the tree that is in the middle of the garden, and you must not touch it, or you will die.'"

"You will not surely die," the serpent said to the woman. "For God knows that when you eat of it your eyes will be opened, and you will be like God, knowing good and evil."

To know good and evil is to be conscious and to be human.

At this point the serpent's role in the temptation ended, and the woman began to rationalize her desire for power through physical, aesthetic, and intellectual reasons for eating the fruit, as Genesis 3:6 tells us:

When the woman saw that the fruit of the tree was good for food and pleasing to the eye, and also desirable for gaining wisdom, she took some and ate it.

Even though the woman was fully alert and remembered what God had said, she was tempted by the desire to be like God and to have God's power.

Temptation comes from within—the serpent is the woman's inner reptile.

The woman wanted to have all the answers and call the shots. For the Hebrews, this was the biggest source of trouble for a human being—the desire to grab spiritual territory from God.

Grabbing territory is something that reptiles and mammals do especially well.

Clearly, the woman did not adequately reflect on the decision she was making. Was the serpent a more trustworthy source of information than God about whether eating the fruit would cause death? Was it really possible for her to be like God by eating a piece of fruit? Was she lost in self-delusion?

The struggle against sin is the struggle to be more conscious.

Apparently, the woman was so overwhelmed by her desire for power that she never reflected on these concerns. She failed to make full use of the cognitive equipment God had given her—and this is a human being's greatest sin.

Use it or lose it. The failure to reflect is the failure to be human.

After indulging herself, the woman immediately reacted by sharing some of the fruit with her husband, as Genesis 3:6 indicates:

She also gave some to her husband, who was with her, and he ate it.

Misery loves company. Sin has a communal aspect to it.

This passage reveals that the man erred even more seriously than the woman. The deal was originally between God and the man, but the man did not even mention it at the moment of temptation. At least the woman remembered the deal. The man didn't seem to use his conscious mind at all in this situation—his acceptance of the fruit was an unconscious reaction to an external stimulus.

If our consciousness is unstable today, how stable was it that long ago?

After eating the forbidden fruit, the man and woman hid from God, afraid of him because of their nakedness. When God asked if they had eaten the forbidden fruit, there was plenty of blame to go around. The man was quick to blame the woman, while the woman blamed the serpent. At least she recognized that she had been deceived, as we read in Genesis 3:11–13:

> And [God] said, "Who told you that you were naked? Have you eaten from the tree that I commanded you not to eat from?"
>
> The man said, "The woman you put here with me—she gave me some fruit from the tree, and I ate it."
>
> Then the Lord God said to the woman, "What is this you have done?"
>
> The woman said, "The serpent deceived me, and I ate."

God told the man and woman that there would be consequences because they had broken the deal. No more Garden of Eden. The woman would endure agonizing childbirth, sexual desire only for her husband, and subordination to her husband. The man would have to give up his genteel role in the garden to perform hard labor. Both would die and return to the dust.

What a guilt trip.

Even the serpent had to pay a penalty—he would have a bad relationship with

Opposite: The ripe fruit of the prickly pear cactus appears in July and is irresistible to many Desert animals.

humans from then on. The Hebrews realized that humans shared an innate fear of snakes, and this story explained why.

However, God acted with compassion toward the man and woman, sewing them clothes out of animal skins so that they would leave the garden adequately clothed.

God is both the just, disciplining father and the loving, compassionate mother. Even so, the image of God using animal skins for their clothing suggests that relationships are no longer the same among God, the Creation, and humanity. The harmony that had existed earlier was shattered by the humans' attempt to have God's power.

After the man and woman leave the garden, they have the names of Adam and Eve—as if the separateness of human existence was a consequence of choosing to eat the forbidden fruit.

Adam and Eve must have left the Garden of Eden with a soul-ache.

The Perfect Fall
. . . . .

In time to come trouble will befall you, because you will do what is evil in the sight of the Lord, provoking him to anger through the work of your hands.

MOSES TO THE HEBREWS, DEUTERONOMY 31:29

Some people think the Adam and Eve story gives women a bad rap. It's the woman's fault; she listened to the serpent and led the man into temptation.

For the ancient Hebrews, this was a reasonable perspective. As far as they could tell, women were merely the vessels for men's seed. Women had to endure unclean monthly bleedings and painful childbirth, while men did not. Women had a more limited sexual appetite than men. They figured that women somehow must have deserved these apparent punishments.

The Hebrews had no idea that a woman contributed so much to the reproductive process. They didn't know about eggs, chromosomes, genes, or mitochondria. They didn't know that the woman's body determines whether a man's sperm is acceptable for reproduction.

They surely didn't know about a woman's larger corpus callosum and the advantage it provides in maintaining consciousness.

However, they understood that women have the edge in staying conscious. Even though Eve was the first to eat the fruit, the story has Adam erring more seriously than Eve.

It's not Eve that gets the bad rap in this story—it is God.

The Adam and Eve story suggests that God reacts to humanity's wrong choices in a very human way. Adam and Eve betrayed God, and God got angry and punished them—isn't that how we would act if someone violated a deal we had made with them?

How could God have gotten so mad at partially evolved humans for messing up?

Unconscious emotions such as fear, anger, and rivalry are commonly mentioned throughout Genesis and the rest of the Old Testament. Since the Hebrews experienced these emotions and believed that they were made in God's image, they sometimes attributed such emotions to God as well.

Although the Hebrews understood that God has a compassionate, merciful side, for them it often seemed to get lost in God's punishing, wrathful behavior.

Little did the Hebrews know how far they had missed the mark with this view of God. Things weren't as bad as they thought in their relationship with God. A kinder, gentler God was patiently waiting for them to see the light.

God was not made in humanity's image, as indicated in this passage from Isaiah 55:8–9, written over twenty-five hundred years ago:

"For my thoughts are not your thoughts,
neither are your ways my ways,"
declares the Lord.
"As the heavens are higher than the earth,
so are my ways higher than your ways
and my thoughts than your thoughts."

Before eating the fruit, Adam and Eve were nameless parts of the Creation. They exercised their freedom to choose, and learned from the consequences of their choice. By doing so, they became self-conscious.

This is what God wanted all along—for a part of the Creation to become self-conscious.

God has known all along about evolution, the primate family tree, and the instability of the human psyche.

God has known all along what is needed for the human mind to realize its potential for consciousness.

Just as soon as humanity was ready, God sent light into the darkness of the human mind through one of the Hebrews' very own.

The word became flesh—the spiritual equivalent of the Big Bang.

I Desire Mercy
. . . . .

For I desire mercy and not sacrifice, the knowledge of God rather than burnt offerings.
GOD, HOSEA 6:6

After nearly two thousand years and enormous amounts of human thought and energy, we still don't know quite what to make of Jesus. He was certainly one of a kind. There has been no one like him, before or since.

Even while he was still alive, there was a tremendous controversy about his identity, one that continues to this day. After all, he had so many identities.

A son, a brother, an artisan.

A prophet, a teacher, a rebel.

A holistic healer, a demon fighter, a miracle worker.

The son of man. The son of God. The word made flesh.

A humble, grateful soultrino magnet. A transformer of dark energy.

While Jesus was not trained as a doctor or a scientist, he understood the human mind better than anyone before or since. He had a gift for bringing out the best in someone's mind.

Like the central message of the Hebrew prophets before him, the teachings of Jesus were fundamentally a call to higher consciousness and spiritual security.

That's good news, all right.

Compared to the authors of the Old Testament, Jesus had a very different perspective on the divine nature. Jesus chose to emphasize the qualities of God that humans experience only through consciousness, such as love, forgiveness, compassion, mercy, rationality, and justice.

Mercy—a disposition to be kind and forgiving. Justice—what is fair for all.

He repeatedly urged everyone around him to pay attention, listen carefully, and not be afraid, but to have faith and believe. He focused on turning away from sin rather than on feeling guilty about sin. Fear and guilt are unconscious emotions, while attention, active listening, faith, and belief are conscious activities. He was teaching his hearers to convert their emotions into feelings, and thereby become more conscious.

> *Therefore consider carefully how you listen. Whoever has will be given more; whoever does not have, even what he thinks he has will be taken from him.*
> JESUS, LUKE 8:18

According to the Gospel of Luke, Jesus began his public ministry by standing up in the synagogue at Nazareth on the Sabbath and reading from the book of the prophet Isaiah. Luke 4:18–19 tells how he read this passage from Isaiah 61:2:

"The Spirit of the Lord is upon me,
because he has anointed me to bring good news to the poor.
He has sent me to proclaim release to the captives
and recovery of sight to the blind,
to let the oppressed go free,
to proclaim the year of the Lord's favor."

Jesus deliberately cut off the last sentence. In Isaiah the sentence ends as follows: "to proclaim the year of the Lord's favor, and the day of vengeance of our God." Jesus was presenting a more loving, compassionate image of God than the Hebrew scriptures offered.

This is not the wrathful, vengeful God of your fathers, folks.

Jesus reflected mercy to everyone around him, regardless of their socioeconomic status. He chastised the priests for being more attentive to religious rituals and laws rather than being merciful to the most needy members of society. Once when reprimanding them, Jesus invoked the words of the prophet Hosea, as Matthew 9:13 shows:

Go and learn what this means, "I desire mercy, not sacrifice."

When praying, Jesus addressed God as "Abba," the equivalent of "Daddy" in the Aramaic dialect of Hebrew in which he spoke. This was a tender, intimate form of address, a form never used in the Old Testament. Not even David, Jesus' ancestor, addressed God in this way, despite his unusually close relationship with God as reflected in the psalms he wrote.

With God as our daddy, how bad can things really be?

The Son of Man

· · · · ·

For the Son of Man came to seek and to save what was lost.
JESUS, LUKE 19:10

Jesus also portrayed God as a loving father applying discipline that is reasonable and fair, albeit at times harsh. However, the underlying motivation for God's justice is always love. Justice and compassion always go together in God—fairness is the divine pruning tool for expanding consciousness and growing more love.

The divine formula for parenting: discipline plus mercy plus affection equals love.

While divine justice will ultimately prevail and hold us accountable for our lives, God's delight is in our success, not our failure. Jesus repeatedly reinforced this point using parables with the theme of the joy one experiences over finding something lost. God does not want to lose us because of our unstable consciousness.

God wants us to be self-conscious—and more.

Jesus wanted the Hebrews—and us—to know that there's something more, something better, beyond this troubled world we live in. There's the kingdom of heaven, where God's will for love, fairness, and peace forges a peaceful harmony for everything and everyone.

It's a good place. A friendly place.

God wants to share that peaceful place with us during our lives here on Earth and forevermore. As Jesus told his disciples in Luke 12:32,

Opposite: This ancient saguaro provides abundant housing for various Desert animals.

In my Father's house are many

rooms; if it were not so,

I would have told you.

I am going there

to prepare a place for you.

<small>JESUS, JOHN 14:2</small>

Do not be afraid, little flock, for it is your Father's good pleasure to give you the kingdom.

It's our choice. We're free to accept or reject God's gracious invitation.

RSVP. Reservations are DEFINITELY *required. No tickets available at the door.*

However, Jesus inferred that we can make this choice only in a state of consciousness. The whole mind must collaborate for us to respond to God's offer. A brain at war with itself cannot make this choice, as Jesus said in Mark 3:24–25:

If a kingdom is divided against itself, that kingdom cannot stand. If a house is divided against itself, that house cannot stand.

No wonder Jesus represented God as loving and compassionate toward us. God knows where we have been, where we are—and where we are going. God knows the whole story for each one of us, and all of us.

God knows about human evolution—back pain, mind games, and soul-ache.

Jesus repeatedly called himself the son of man and rarely called himself the son of God in the Gospels of Mark, Matthew, and Luke. The phrase "son of man" also appeared in the Old Testament in the books of Ezekiel and Daniel, written several hundred years before Jesus was born.

Daniel 7:13 reveals a vision of a different sort of human than the Hebrews were used to:

I saw one like a son of man coming with the clouds of heaven. And he came to the Ancient One and was presented before him.

Since Jesus was very familiar with the Old Testament, he was surely aware of these references. But of all the images in the Old Testament, why did he latch onto this one to describe himself?

The son of man. What comes after man.

Jesus was living proof of the evolution of human consciousness. There's something other than our current level of consciousness that is the highest state available to the human mind. Whatever it's called—cosmic consciousness, spiritual enlightenment, the Tao, whatever—Jesus had it. Big time.

God offered him a mental room with a view—and he took it.

Jesus lived in the kingdom of heaven while he was on Earth. In this state of king-dom consciousness, the universe can be only a friendly place. Thankfully, that's what God and Jesus want for all of us.

God and Jesus do not close the kingdom to anyone—only people do that.

Jesus said that knowing the truth would set us free. But he forgot to tell us some-thing. What did he mean? The truth about what will set us free from what?

Now evolution has taught us what he meant: the truth about ourselves will set us free from ourselves. And once we are free from *ourselves,* we will truly be free, for all eternity.

Free will: we get to choose whether to be like a reptile, a mammal, or a human.

> *Along with the consciousness of the cosmos there occurs an intellectual enlightenment or illumination which alone . . . would make him almost a member of a new species.*
> RICHARD MAURICE BUCKE, *Cosmic Consciousness*

company
. . . . .

For thousands of years, civilization's spiritual geniuses from around the world have been pointing us toward a higher level of consciousness. Now, we can under-stand better what they have been trying to tell us.

Evolution is not an abstract theory that enables us to understand and control the world around and within us. Evolution is a force of Nature that hasn't stopped just because we now know about it. All life is subject to evolution—including us.

Especially us.

Through evolution, God and the universe seem intent on delivering fully con-scious human beings. Our abilities to transform emotions into feelings and think symbolically hold the key to our humanity and consciousness.

Consciousness leads away from violence and toward spiritual security.

However, a major obstacle to the evolution of human consciousness is that the unconscious and conscious minds have very different needs—and we are not always good at even recognizing them, let alone balancing them, because the conscious mind is prone to isolation and delusion.

The unconscious mind yearns for time in Nature, fresh air, sunshine, exercise, proper nutrition, adequate rest and relaxation, and minimal interference from foreign substances. It longs for a chance to indulge curiosity and imagination—even in adults. The unconscious mind considers stopping to smell the roses a form of work, not play.

However, the conscious mind has other priorities. For its own imagined rewards, it selfishly exposes the unconscious mind and the body to various forms of slavery, such as long daily commutes, sitting indoors for long periods, eating junk food, frequent stressful interactions, unnecessary surgeries and drugs, and substance abuse.

In postindustrial society, slavery has become self-inflicted.

This is self-destructive behavior, since the unconscious mind runs the show physically and mentally. For some reason, the conscious mind often likes to pretend that it didn't arise from Nature and is not subject to its demands and constraints.

> *It is hard to have a Southern overseer;*
> *it is worse to have a Northern one;*
> *but worst of all when you are the*
> *slave-driver of yourself.*
> HENRY DAVID THOREAU, *Walden*

The ultimate act of consciousness is to assist with our own evolution. So how do we go forward?

How do we find ways to live and work that achieve the right balance among experience, intellect, and intuition? How do we find ways to live and work that accommodate the mind, the body, and the soul?

How do we experience stable self-consciousness, let alone go beyond that?

Most importantly, how do we help our children become more conscious than we are?

Are children more or less conscious than adults today?

Fortunately, the answers are around us and within us. God is on our side, and wants us to succeed. God has known all along that this is a big job—too big for us to handle by ourselves.

God knew before the Big Bang that we would need help to be fully conscious and to see the universe as a friendly place.

God has known all along that the only hope for us is company.

All kinds of company—divine, human, and otherwise.

Especially the Desert's company.

. . . . .

And I have by me, for my comfort, two strange white flowers . . .
to witness that even when mind and strength had gone,
gratitude and a mutual tenderness still lived on in the heart of man.
H. G. WELLS, *The Time Machine*

FIVE

community

Then the Lord said to Cain, "Where is your brother Abel?" He said, "I do not know; am I my brother's keeper?" And the Lord said, "What have you done? Listen, your brother's blood is crying out to me from the ground!"

GENESIS 4:9–10

And pointing to his disciples, he said, "Here are my mother and my brothers! For whoever does the will of my Father in heaven is my brother and sister and mother."

JESUS, MATTHEW 12:49–50

For the whole law is summed up in a single commandment, "You shall love your neighbor as yourself." If, however, you bite and devour one another, take care that you are not consumed by one another.

PAUL, GALATIANS 5:14–15

The highest possible stage in moral culture is when we recognize that we ought to control our thoughts.

CHARLES DARWIN, *The Descent of Man*

Opposite: The Hohokam communicated with one another and other tribes with rock art—art etched onto rocks and boulders.

*L*ate one April night a couple of years ago, strange sounds from the Desert drifted in through an open window. Digging, munching, grunting, snorting, and woofing sounds.

Dawn revealed the culprits: a herd of twelve adult javelinas. These large mammals, also known as collared peccaries, are named for their sharp, javelin-like tusks, which allow them to eat the tough, juicy roots of cacti and agaves.

Although they look like pigs and are often called pigs, they are more closely related to horses and rats than to pigs. They are relative newcomers to this Desert, as there is little archaeological evidence of them prior to the 1700s. Originally from South America, they probably traveled up the land bridge through Central America well before the Panama Canal was an obstacle.

Although their character is about as ornery as the plants they eat, javelinas are inexplicably mesmerizing and amusing. They grunt and moan with delight when they're eating something good. In the winter they often curl up together after a meal, with the babies' heads sticking up out of the flesh pile.

In several prior years, we had seen only a couple of javelinas, and those rarely. Typically a herd has a territory of five hundred to one thousand acres that it patrols and prunes regularly. In the past, our area had seemed to be beyond their normal range. But that spring, a prolonged drought was driving them to expand their territory to stay alive.

That morning the javelinas were spread out nearby over a half acre or so in groups of two or three, feasting on prickly pear cacti and digging to uncover the stubborn, meaty roots that no other critter can eat. Occasionally two would line up head to tail and affectionately rub each other with obvious delight as they reapplied their strong, musky scent to one another to affirm their communal bond.

The clan that rubs together stays together.

After a few minutes the herd of pigs vanished into the Desert right before my eyes, like steam from a boiling kettle disappearing into the air. They were headed down to their version of a highway—a densely foliated wash—to continue their travels and adventures.

But one stayed behind. This was a large, gnarly, older javelina who was sprawled

on the ground, munching on a particularly well-endowed cactus. When she got up, her first few steps revealed a serious impairment somewhere in the vicinity of her left hip. Her stride was slow and awkward, but she didn't appear to be in pain or bleeding. Perhaps this was some old injury from a car or a bullet, or the effect of a debilitating disease like arthritis.

All the other javelinas had already taken off and left this poor Old Girl behind. She was a sorry sight to see, crippled and alone in the Desert.

Above: While javelinas can be very dangerous, they are generally good natured and beguiling.

Surprisingly, she hobbled slowly over to the side yard to check out the cacti there—in the opposite direction from that in which the herd had departed. Was she lost, greedy, or stupid? Would she be able to catch up to the herd with her cumbersome gait?

Old Girl didn't find anything of interest in the side yard. Finally, she seemed to show some concern about reuniting with the herd, as if she had caught a whiff of a coyote, bobcat, or mountain lion. She put her nose up in the air, took a few steps, then sniffed again. After a few false starts, she turned and walked down the exact same path the herd had taken to the nearby wash.

Slowly Old Girl walked through scrubby brush, dragging her lame hindquarters behind her without complaint. She no longer stopped for cactus, but kept moving forward to catch up to her distant companions.

As she hobbled off into the Desert, Old Girl seemed to tell the story of us all: continually yearning for the freedom to pursue our desires, yet always drawn back to the security and constraints of the herd, haunted by our wounds, predators, and delusions.

Eventually we learned that everything had worked out fine that day for Old Girl. She came back in early August, this time with two handsome babies and only six adult companions. They were starving, since the cacti they feed on were dying owing to meager summer rains.

This Desert has always been hard on animal communities—especially human ones.

And human communities have tended to be hard on this Desert.

Those Who Have Gone
. . . . .

What finally became of them? Who knows? One by one they passed away, or perhaps were all slaughtered in a night.
JOHN C. VAN DYKE, *The Desert*

Because of this Desert's intense heat and difficult living conditions, few Americans came to live here after Arizona was admitted to the union in 1912 as the forty-eighth state.

A latecomer with a checkered past.

The proliferation of air conditioning after World War II changed all that. Gradually people began coming to the Desert. They liked it, and they stayed. Their families and friends visited, and they moved here, too. Soon a population boom was in full swing.

Since the early 1980s, Arizona has been making up for lost time in terms of population growth. Governmental entities such as Maricopa County, Pima County, Phoenix, Scottsdale, and Tucson have approved numerous leapfrog developments that have compromised the existence of many species in this fragile Desert community.

They paved paradise and put up the red-tile roofs.

Then again, Arizona has always been a boom-and-bust kind of place. This latest population boom is not the first. Long before Columbus arrived in the New World, an extended population growth spurt began and eventually ended in a baffling disaster.

The most successful pre-Columbian inhabitants of this area were the Hohokam, known for their sophisticated irrigation system and prosperous civilization. These foothills around us, just north of the Salt River Valley, were full of settlements and cropland.

Maybe too full.

Based on the plentiful ruins and artifacts in our area, it appears that the Hohokam had a good thing going—while it lasted. They had a distinctive culture in this area by AD 400, and they thrived from AD 600 to 1000. But by the year 1200, something had gone terribly wrong for them. By the year 1400, they had vanished altogether.

When the Spanish arrived in this area in the early 1500s, all that was left of the Hohokam was their ruins. Their former neighbors, the Pima Indians, called them the *Hohokam*—from the Pima words for "those who have gone" or "those who are all used up."

In the late 1800s, the Hohokam canals were discovered and utilized once again for irrigation. The new city that arose from the ashes of the Hohokam was named

Phoenix, after the mythical bird that burned itself to ashes, then rose from the ashes to live again.

Will Phoenix self-destruct once again—or learn to collaborate with the Desert?

Archaeological evidence suggests that over the last three hundred years of its existence Hohokam society became riddled with problems, including violence, invasion, natural catastrophes, ecological setbacks, and socioeconomic polarization. Their slow demise was marked by two distinct trends: increasingly luxurious housing for leaders and the decline of traditional artistic and religious practices.

Although the cause of the Hohokam's collapse is still uncertain, there are several theories about what happened to them.

Some evidence suggests that an aggressive tribe from Central America migrated north to escape drought or social collapse and destabilized Hohokam society. This theory is consistent with the stories handed down by the Pima Indians, which indicate that warfare and migration destroyed the Hohokam.

Another possibility is that a double whammy of major floods and long droughts strained the Hohokam's canals and social institutions to the breaking point. Or the Hohokam might have created an ecological disaster by devegetating the Desert and diverting natural runoff into their canals.

Most likely it was a combination of these factors that finished off the Hohokam. Whatever happened, an inadequate water supply seemed to have had something to do with their demise.

And it just might have something to do with ours.

Millions of years ago, drought gave birth to the Sonoran Desert. Since then, it has continually threatened her survival. In 2002, we learned this lesson first-hand. A four-year drought had taken a heavy toll on this Desert. Even highly drought-resistant residents like prickly pear cactus and the thorny shrubs called ocotillos began to shrivel up and die.

The saguaros got thinner and started to drop limbs—yet surprised everyone with a bumper crop of blossoms. In response to hard times, these native Sonoran

Opposite: The holes in this ancient boulder were formed centuries ago as the Hohokam ground grain into flour.

stalwarts produce even more offspring to replace those that are going to die. Indeed, the saguaros were right. They knew what was coming. Many of them died a slow death over the following months.

Are we as good as the saguaros in anticipating what's coming?

Some evidence suggests that the Hohokam may have experienced a drought for as long as thirty years. Imagine the anguish they would have endured as they watched the drought, like a very slow-moving fire, consume everything that was important right before their eyes: their canals and crops, the Desert's plants and animals, their society's institutions, their children and loved ones, and finally their own bodies and souls.

The moon and the mountains remember the agonizing cries of their starving babies.

At some point during their long decline, the Hohokam must have finally realized that it was not their leaders who called the shots—it was the climate. No rain, no food. Too much rain, no food. But by then it was probably too late for them to right the wrongs of several centuries. After the hard times ended, the Desert bounced back—but they did not.

So the Hohokam learned about community the hard way. Just as we all must.

The question is "Why?"

Most of the luxuries, and many of the so-called comforts of life, are not only not indispensable, but positive hindrances to the elevation of mankind. . . . What makes families run out? What is the nature of the luxury which enervates and destroys nations? Are we sure that there is none of it in our own lives?
HENRY DAVID THOREAU, *Walden*

Despite repeated disasters, biotic communities like the Desert can persist for millions of years. We are supposed to be the smartest animals ever to have walked the Earth. So why is it that our civilizations' prosperity is generally measured in centuries and not in millennia?

Why have the Hohokam and most other civilizations followed the same pattern—formation, success, crisis, decline, and collapse—over several hundred years?

How have the cosmic forces of self-destruction and collaboration influenced civilization?

Why has dark energy always succeeded in making civilizations self-destructive?

What role has civilization played in the development of human consciousness? Is it helping or hindering the expansion of consciousness today?

We need each other to figure out where we are, and how to go forward.

At least that's what the universe has been trying to tell us.

When will the drought in our minds end?

The mind of the universe is social.
MARCUS AURELIUS, *Meditations*

Come Together
. . . . .

A community is a group of individuals that shares similar interests. To be in community is to associate, to be in relationship—either in a warm and fuzzy way or in a nasty and brutish way.

From early on, inanimate parts of the cosmos have demonstrated a predisposition to group life, thanks to destructive collisions and gravitational attraction. Particles combine into atoms. Atoms group into molecules. Molecules clump into elements. Elements form stars. Planets orbit around stars. Moons orbit around planets. Stars cluster in galaxies. Galaxies bunch together.

Earth is the greatest cosmic experiment in building community. Here the inanimate and the animate are integrated so seamlessly that it is difficult to determine where one stops and the other starts.

As with the rest of the universe, life on Earth has tended to stick together in groups. Over three billion years ago, simple microbes began living in colonies. Amid the unpredictable conditions on Earth, clearly there were better odds of physical survival in groups. Yet their success exposed them to the genetic variation that produced the self-destructive cheater cell.

The purpose of community in Nature is to facilitate physical survival.

Evolution seems to have deliberately encouraged interaction and collaboration. All species, regardless of their habitats, sociability, intelligence, or complexity, are forced into biotic communities by their instincts to consume resources and reproduce. The smartest species, such as primates and marine mammals, are highly social and cooperative.

The purpose of evolution is to encourage collaboration.

Early human ancestors of the genus *Homo* were social and communal, pioneering a nomadic hunter-gatherer group lifestyle that endured for almost two million years. Their approach to community was not so different from that of other social mammals: Live with your blood relatives. Might makes right. Find enough food for everyone. Keep the babies coming. Travel light.

To take care of only your own clan is mammalian behavior.

However, evolution's most impressive and risky venture in the attempt to encourage community was civilization—and the world has never been quite the same since.

Fast Forward
· · · · ·

The friendly and flowing savage, who is he?
Is he waiting for civilization, or past it and mastering it?
WALT WHITMAN, *"Song of Myself"*

The term *civilization* comes from the Latin word for citizen and describes a condition of human society marked by significant activity in the arts and sciences as well as social, cultural, and political institutions.

To be civilized is to be orderly, creative, and polite.

Although civilization is a relatively recent development in human history, it has played an important role in the expansion of human consciousness.

Agriculture, the catalyst of civilization, was feasible only after the last ice age subsided. Over ten thousand years ago, after the enormous floods caused by melting ice had subsided, agriculture began to provide a more attractive alternative for securing food than hunting and gathering.

The first permanent agrarian settlements sprouted in the mild, favorable conditions of Mesopotamia (modern-day Iraq). These small villages represented the first human attempts at forming a community based on shared interests, beliefs, and territory rather than on kinship and clan. Horticulture and domestic animals became an important part of daily life.

Plants and domestic animals helped to civilize us.

This new agrarian lifestyle required more frequent human interaction on a daily basis, which apparently spurred the blossoming of modern languages. New forms of communication stimulated human consciousness in a way that was not possible for those living a more nomadic lifestyle.

For our hunter-gatherer ancestors, certain aspects of the conscious mind would have been more useful than others. The vision skills of the occipital region and the movement and orientation skills of the parietal region would have been very helpful in handling the challenges of living in Nature. Not coincidentally, these are also the oldest areas of the cortex.

However, the listening and speech skills of the temporal lobe and the feeling and symbolic-thought skills of the frontal lobe were probably of relatively little use to hunter-gatherers owing to the more solitary and uncertain nature of existence. Women probably led a more interactive lifestyle than men because of their child-raising duties.

Agrarian living probably had a stimulating effect on the temporal and frontal areas of the cortex. The development of modern spoken language and frequent human interaction must have placed great demands on the temporal lobe. In addition, the planning skills that are crucial to success in agriculture probably challenged the frontal lobe in unprecedented ways.

I see the constructiveness of my race,
I see ranks, colors, barbarisms, civilizations,
I go among them, I mix indiscriminately,
And I salute all the inhabitants of the earth.
WALT WHITMAN, *"Salut au Monde!"*

During the Bronze Age (3500–1000 BC), the world's first major civilizations formed in different parts of the world: Egypt, Central America (the Mayans), China, Egypt, the Middle East (Sumeria), and South America (the Incas). All of these groups successfully used celestial movements to help predict planting seasons and generate significant stores of food and wealth, which gave some people more leisure time to pursue creative and intellectual activities rather than simply perform daily labor.

Dark skies helped to stimulate the frontal lobe and enrich civilization.

Several key developments at this time would have galvanized the expansion of the conscious mind, including the advent of:

Timekeeping (first calendar used in Egypt 4000 BC)

Mathematics (first numbers used in Egypt 3000 BC)

Advanced storytelling (the Gilgamesh Epic first told
in Sumeria 3000 BC)

Writing (cuneiform first used in Sumeria 3000 BC)

Moral standards (the Ten Commandments in the Middle East 1200 BC)

The purpose of civilization is to personalize the impersonal aspects of existence.

Although it is impossible to tell when the cortex started specializing language functions on the left side, it probably would not have bothered with such a difficult task before the development of written language. Writing and reading placed significant new demands on the cortex and probably encouraged greater overall mental efficiency for less complex tasks.

Thinking, feeling, speaking, and writing created civilization. Ignorance and cruelty threaten it.

Some have speculated that the literary works of Homer in ancient Greece some 3,000 years ago were the first indication of a modern cortex with a specialized side for language functions (the left brain for most people).

"All the same," said the Scarecrow, "I shall ask for brains instead of a heart; for a fool would not know what to do with a heart if he had one." "I shall take the heart," returned the Tin Woodman; "for brains do not make one happy, and happiness is the best thing in the world."
L. FRANK BAUM, *The Wizard of Oz*

Since the onset of civilization, it is clear that increasing human interaction has exponentially expanded consciousness. This is strikingly obvious when you consider that it took our species about 70,000 years to first start wearing clothes, but only about 5,000 years to go from written language to the Internet!

Has civilization enabled conscious feelings and happiness to grow at this same pace?

Today it is just as obvious that civilization is at a crossroads, and that it cannot continue much longer in its current direction.

> *While civilization has been improving our houses, it has not*
> *equally improved the men who are to inhabit them.*
> HENRY DAVID THOREAU, *Walden*

Given the stimulating effect on consciousness, you would think that civilizations would flourish for many millennia. But this is not the case.

Civilization has had a somewhat checkered past. The most enduring civilizations have lasted only between one and two thousand years, and have often experienced long periods of decline before collapsing altogether.

What is it that makes civilizations sputter and die? Social scientists cite many common factors, among them a lack of fresh water, desertification of cropland, inadequate high-quality protein, social unrest, political corruption, institutional collapse, and violent conflicts with enemies.

Underlying many of these problems is a common symptom: a selfish inclination to grab and defend resources that spins out of control in some members of the community.

It's the same problem the microbes had with the cheater cell over three billion years ago!

Although a territorial instinct is innate to human nature, it appears that permanent settlements gave this ancient urge a new arena for expression. Prior to the development of agriculture, hunter-gatherers moved around seasonally along with their food sources, and maintained few possessions so they could travel light.

> *A spider is proud when it has caught a fly;*
> *so is a man when he has caught a hare,*
> *another when he has taken a fish in a net,*
> *another when he has killed wild boars or*
> *bears, another when he has captured*
> *Sarmatians. Are they not all brigands,*
> *if you look into their principles?*
> MARCUS AURELIUS, *Meditations*

Although they had social hierarchies, generally there was economic equality. They left behind some evidence of fighting that suggested violence between both individuals and groups, but nothing quite like the wars perpetrated after the appearance of agriculture.

Some early archaeological evidence of war dates to the same time and place as the earliest agricultural settlements—about 8000 BC in Mesopotamia. Thereafter,

Do you not see the little plants, the little birds, the ants, the spiders, the bees, working together to set in order their several parts of the universe? And are you unwilling to do the work of a human being, not eager to do what belongs to your nature?

MARCUS AURELIUS, *Meditations*

war became a part of daily life around the world. Early civilizations also left behind evidence of socioeconomic polarization.

Given what we now know about human evolution, the agrarian lifestyle must have provoked a very mammalian territorial instinct—one that is still easily observed throughout the world today.

Big crops, big house, big harem, big kahuna—any mammal could understand this.

However, other mammals do not seem to share our tendency to acquire resources far beyond what is needed—they know when enough is enough.

Somehow, the expansion of human consciousness, combined with an aroused mammalian territorial instinct, has delivered an unprecedented level of violence and death to civilization's doorstep—particularly over the past hundred years. Despite the obvious threat of weapons of mass destruction, we have still not yet figured out how to reconcile the potent force of consciousness with our mammalian instincts.

As a result, civilization as we know it today seems to be more self-destructive than collaborative. This dilemma is abundantly obvious here in one of civilization's greatest experiments ever, the United States of America.

The Land of the Free
. . . . .

Most men, even in this comparatively free country, through mere ignorance and mistake, are so occupied with the factitious cares and superfluously coarse labors of life that its finer fruits cannot be plucked by them.
HENRY DAVID THOREAU, *Walden*

Among the many past and present nations of the world, the United States has enjoyed unprecedented levels of freedom, talent, and wealth, particularly since the end of World War II.

After the war, American business met global demand using management techniques similar to those that had helped win the war. Institutions advanced on

Opposite: Organpipe cactus blossoms attract several different pollinators.

many fronts in American society—despite Americans' innate distrust of institutions, a trait that can be traced back to our founding fathers.

The good news is that the United States has developed preeminent institutions in a wide range of fields. The bad news is that these powerful institutions have become too good at doing the wrong things.

Just as happened with the Hohokam and others—institutions became a feeding ground for the greedy.

On January 17, 1961, President Dwight D. Eisenhower warned against institutional abuses of power in his often-quoted farewell address:

> This conjunction of an immense military establishment and a large arms industry is new in the American experience. The total influence—economic, political, even spiritual—is felt in every city, every statehouse, every office of the federal government. In the councils of government, we must guard against the acquisition of unwarranted influence, whether sought or unsought, by the military-industrial complex. The potential for the disastrous rise of misplaced power exists and will persist.

Eisenhower called those who sought such influence the "merchants of death," and he warned that they would be encouraging the United States to wage war, to help their corporate bottom lines. Since his warning, various wars—including those in Korea, Vietnam, Afghanistan, and Iraq—have indeed enriched American corporations even as they have taken many lives.

Surely even Eisenhower would have been shocked at how right he was. The "disastrous rise of misplaced power" that he foresaw didn't stop with the military-industrial complex. It metastasized throughout American society like a deadly tumor, one that has become painfully obvious in these early years of the new millennium.

Government leaders exploiting national assets and commercializing regulatory functions.

Clergy members molesting children and committing adultery and embezzlement.

Doctors widely prescribing drugs with insufficient evidence of their benefits and risks.

Business leaders distorting financial results and the threat of global warming.

Intelligence leaders fighting turf wars rather than attending to national security.

What happened here in the land of the free?

Houston, we've got a problem.

Since the end of World War II, American society has become obsessed with the human mind's most primitive desires: pleasure, security, social status, and tangible rewards. Many trends have stimulated this obsession, including the growth of such visual media as television, movies, and magazines; the urbanization of America; the proliferation of weapons of mass destruction; and economic and cultural globalization.

Despite all her achievements, America has not avoided falling into the same trap as other civilizations. Our most valuable assets—human talent and natural resources—have been greatly exploited over the past sixty years to enrich a relatively small sliver of society.

No wonder American politics has become so divisive.

> *I cannot believe that our factory system is the best mode by which men may get clothing. . . . The principal object is not that mankind may be well and honestly clad but, unquestionably, that the corporations may be enriched.*
> HENRY DAVID THOREAU, *Walden*

While many Americans have benefited from a rising economic tide to at least some degree, the ranks of those who have been left behind grow daily—the uninsured, the homeless, the undereducated, the unemployed and underemployed. Today American society is choking on the hoards of illegal immigrants who provide the cheap labor that wealthy Americans and businesses crave.

America has always had an unseemly appetite for cheap labor, beginning with African slaves.

Now it is America's turn to face the age-old threats of socioeconomic polarization, social decline, and ecological disaster.

We in America, and civilization as a whole, need more leaders who can show us how to become more conscious, and do so quickly—leaders who can help us pull back from the brink of self-destruction and teach us to collaborate better.

Over the past five thousand years, civilization has produced many examples of the way to pursue either self-destruction or collaboration. The ancient Hebrews have been a good source on both sides of the ledger.

The Desert helps the human mind choose life over death.

All in the Family
. . . . .

Then Abram said to Lot, "Let there be no strife between you and me, and between your herders and my herders; for we are kindred."
GENESIS 13:8

From the time of Abraham, the ancient Hebrews were always a clannish bunch. For them, the concerns of the group—be it family, tribe, or kingdom—were more important than the needs of the individual. Each person's fortunes rose or fell with those of the group, making duty to the group a high priority.

However, they were also aware that living in groups had a tendency to bring out both the best and the worst in people.

The Hebrews believed that, because humans were made in God's image, they were capable of choosing to do right by God and others. However, they were confounded by the widespread human inclination toward sin, whereby one willfully chooses to do the wrong thing—particularly in the form of violence. They knew that sin infects both physical and spiritual reality.

Sin comes naturally to us because of our mammalian instincts.

While the Adam and Eve story addresses the individual's unwillingness to accept limits on his or her freedom, the story of Cain and Abel illustrates how sin and violence affect the human community.

One day Cain and Abel, the sons of Adam and Eve, both offered sacrifices to God. God had a high regard for Abel and his sacrifice, but not for Cain and his sacrifice. Cain became angry.

The dark energy of anger tempts us toward self-destruction.

In Genesis 4:6–7 God had a counseling session with Cain and tried to reason with him:

> Why are you angry, and why has your countenance fallen? If you do well, will you not be accepted? And if you do not do well, sin is lurking at the door; its desire is for you, but you must master it.

Despite Cain's outward religiosity as indicated by his sacrifice, he didn't miss a beat in ignoring God's advice. He immediately went out to the field with Abel and killed him, thus claiming for himself God's power over life and death.

Sin and suffering exist because personal freedom exists.

Cain attempted to hide the truth from God with his infamous wisecrack about being his brother's keeper, but God knew the truth and held Cain accountable for what he had done in Genesis 4:11–12:

> And now you are cursed from the ground, which has opened its mouth to receive your brother's blood from your hand. When you till the ground, it will no longer yield to you its strength; you will be a fugitive and a wanderer on the earth.

Clearly, the Hebrews saw responsibility toward the human community as part of the order of Creation. For them, to sin against another person was not only wrong, but also disruptive of the divine order of Creation. As a result, the sinner was alienated from the whole community—including God, the Creation, others, and self.

Sin depersonalizes existence and brings loneliness and soul-ache.

When Cain complained that in his outcast state he would be vulnerable to others who might wish to kill him, God responded that he would protect Cain with a special mark—even though Cain had expressed no remorse for his sin. Just as God gave Adam and Eve tunics of skins to cover their physical nakedness, God covered Cain's social nakedness in an act of undeserved kindness, or grace.

Cain went on to do good things, and eventually became the father of those who founded the first cities. This suggests a belief that people are redeemable despite their sinful nature.

But the Hebrews had more than stories to assist their communal struggle to understand and combat sin. They employed a formidable weapon against unethical behavior: a guide to morality called the law.

The Law
. . . . .

> *Moses then took the blood, sprinkled it on the people and said, "This is the blood of the covenant that the Lord has made with you in accordance with all these words."*
>
> EXODUS 24:8

As we saw in Chapter Two, God and Abraham forged an unprecedented arrangement called a covenant. This covenant applied not only to Abraham but also to his descendants—the clan. The simple terms were framed by God: You will be my people, and I will be your God.

The most dramatic expression of this covenant occurred when the Hebrews were miraculously liberated from captivity in Egypt under the leadership of Moses. This event, the Exodus, is commemorated by the important Jewish holiday of Passover.

After their liberation around 1250 BC, God instructed Moses to lead the Hebrews through the Sinai Desert. This was a very difficult time for the Hebrews, as they wandered restlessly and suffered from hunger and thirst. They complained bitterly to Moses, resentful that God would deliver them from bondage in Egypt to live in such privation. This wandering continued for forty years.

Why did God want them to live with such hardship for so long?

God had a good reason. God sent the Hebrews into the Desert to help them expand their consciousness without the distractions of civilization, and to prepare them for a revolutionary approach to morality: the Ten Commandments.

God wanted to infuse them with soultrinos.

Living in slavery for many generations would have muted the Hebrews' sense

Opposite: Like the Sinai Desert and other deserts around the world, the Sonoran Desert includes rugged areas with minimal vegetation and severe landscapes.

Every valley shall be raised up,

every mountain and hill made low;

the rough ground shall become level,

the rugged places a plain.

And the glory of the Lord will be revealed,

and all mankind together will see it.

For the mouth of the Lord has spoken.

Isaiah 40:4–5

of control over life and dulled their consciousness. What could be more conducive to building consciousness than being outside, walking, interacting frequently in their native tongue, and addressing new challenges to stay alive without the distractions of possessions, territory, and farming? Forty years would also have been long enough for a new generation untainted by slavery to arise, as those who had escaped from Egypt died off.

The Sinai Desert setting for this sojourn was no coincidence. The sunshine, warm temperatures, dry air, starry nights, dramatic vistas, and severe landscape of sand and rock would also have been stimulating to the human cortex.

God was using the Desert to promote their spiritual exfoliation.

Most important, the Desert revealed the truth about this world for the Hebrews: it was territory hostile for the human soul. They could not survive spiritually in the world without God's help, as Moses reminded them in Deuteronomy 8:3–5:

> He humbled you, causing you to hunger and then feeding you with manna,
> which neither you nor your fathers had known, to teach you that man does not
> live on bread alone but by every word that comes from the mouth of the Lord.
> Your clothes did not wear out and your feet did not swell during these forty years.
> Know then in your heart that as a man disciplines his son, so the Lord your God
> disciplines you.

After this extended Desert therapy, God gave the Hebrews a set of simple rules for living—the Ten Commandments. When this code was introduced over three thousand years ago, its moral coherence was unprecedented in human history, and it remains a potent force to this day.

After sharing the commandments with the Hebrews, Moses (quoted in Deuteronomy 6:4–7) instructed them to maintain conscious attention to their covenant with God and the Ten Commandments:

> Hear, O Israel: The Lord our God, the Lord is one. Love the Lord your God with
> all your heart and with all your soul and with all your strength. These command-
> ments I give to you today are to be upon your hearts. Impress them on your chil-
> dren. Talk about them when you sit at home and when you walk along the road,
> when you lie down and when you get up.

Shortly thereafter, the Hebrews settled down in the Promised Land. Their leaders created a religious institution that had not been feasible during their Desert sojourn, one that placed priests in Moses' role as the intermediary between God and the people of God. As Hebrew society flourished, the priests used their important status for personal financial gain.

Although the Ten Commandments were the principal guidelines for living under the covenant, more detailed guidance was needed for daily life. The Hebrew religious leaders created a compelling combination of stories, teachings, history, and do's and don'ts that are today found along with the Ten Commandments in the first five books of the Old Testament (also called the Torah or the law): Genesis, Exodus, Leviticus, Numbers, and Deuteronomy.

While Moses was traditionally considered the author of these books, it is now clear that several contributors and editors helped to shape the writings over more than a thousand years. The Torah and the rest of the Old Testament were not in final form until about AD 100, when they were officially canonized (declared sacred) in response to the development of Christianity and the Hebrews' dispersion from the Middle East.

Even a cursory look at the books of Exodus, Leviticus, Numbers, and Deuteronomy reveals an obsession with rules, rituals, and sacrifices. Some of the rules seem immoral by today's standards, such as the one in Leviticus 21:9:

> If a priest's daughter defiles herself by becoming a prostitute, she disgraces her father; she must be burned in the fire.

While there are valuable teachings in these books, the complexity of the regulations almost guaranteed noncompliance. Since illiteracy was common in those days, the Hebrews were totally dependent on their religious leaders to tell them how to stay in right relationship with God, and what sacrifices were needed to make amends with God for sin.

Would that all the Lord's people were prophets, and that the Lord would put his spirit on them!
MOSES, NUMBERS 11:29

Many years earlier, Moses had yearned for God to be in direct contact with people—as if he had known that the law and its priests were not going to be enough by themselves. Indeed, they weren't.

God knew that the Hebrews would need something more than the law and priests to help them expand consciousness and collaborate personally with God.

As soon as civilization was ready, a new spiritual leader arrived to show people how to have a more up-close and personal relationship with God.

The New Deal
. . . . .

I have eagerly desired to eat this Passover with you before I suffer.
For I tell you, I will not eat it again until it finds fulfillment
in the kingdom of God.
JESUS, LUKE 22:15–16

Jesus' birth coincided with a unique period in world history. The great Greek and Roman civilizations had formed empires that made significant contributions to humanity and that raised human consciousness to a new level.

The Greeks were responsible for profound advances in language, philosophy, oration, the arts, science, and other areas that are strongly correlated to temporal and frontal activity. Less intellectually and aesthetically inclined, the Romans were masters of administration and building, pursuits that draw heavily on occipital and parietal activity. Their skill at shaping structures extended from roads to aqueducts to human institutions.

The Romans were smart enough to maintain Greek as the common language of the Roman Empire, which extended throughout Europe and the Middle East and into Africa and Asia. Because of that common language—as well as the network of roads, the efficient system of administration, and the maintenance of peace under the Empire—the exchange of goods and ideas occurred at an unprecedented pace. Such exchange would have been highly stimulating to the development of consciousness.

Theirs was an Internet made up of roads, hooves, feet, and letters.

However, all these benefits came at a price. The Romans' vast empire was built upon one of the most oppressive and brutal regimes in history.

At the time Jesus was born, the Hebrew religious leaders enjoyed an uneasy coexistence with the local Roman representatives. They frequently wavered between submission and resistance as they struggled with their nationalistic and mammalian inclinations. Although these leaders were adept at extracting material gain from their fellow Hebrews, they did not take too kindly to the Romans pulling the same trick on them.

This was the perfect moment in time for the arrival of a messenger with a revolutionary message: God wants us to build a new kind of human community under a new covenant.

Building on the teachings of the law and the prophets, Jesus forged a new covenant to liberate the human heart from guilt over breaking the law and fear of God's punishment. He showed how these primitive emotions could be transcended through a conscious effort to partner with God in daily life.

Under this new covenant between God and the people of God, the individual's responsibility was to acknowledge mistakes and sin, and then move beyond them to see new and better ways to act—repentance. Daily personal reflection and prayer were a central part of relating to God, rather than reliance on human intermediaries. A humble, contrite heart was the only sacrifice needed under the new covenant.

Most importantly, spirituality was to be expressed in daily life, rather than through rituals at the temple. The members of the community were responsible for reflecting conscious feelings, such as love, mercy, fairness, patience, and forgiveness, in their dealings with others—even those outside their community. They were to help each other remember Jesus' personal sacrifice to secure the new covenant through a ritualistic shared meal, or communion.

The sacrifice acceptable to God
is a broken spirit;
a broken and contrite heart,
O God, you will not despise.
DAVID, PSALM 51:17 NRSV

The purpose of rituals is to help us remember where we have been—and where we are going.

This new covenant was made under very different conditions from the old covenant. While Moses had been a military, political, and spiritual leader to his

The people walking in darkness have seen a great light;
on those living in the land of the shadow of death
  a light has dawned.
For to us a child is born, to us a son is given,
and the government will be on his shoulders.
And he will be called Wonderful Counselor, Mighty God,
Everlasting Father, Prince of Peace.

Isaiah 9:2,6

people, Jesus was strictly a spiritual leader. The blood that had sealed the old covenant had been that of a hapless sacrificial lamb or other animal, but the new covenant was sealed by the blood of a fully conscious person willing to die to accomplish God's plan, as confirmed in Matthew 26:27–28:

> Then he took the cup, gave thanks and offered it to them, saying, "Drink from it, all of you. This is my blood of the covenant, which is poured out for many for the forgiveness of sins."

For the law was given through Moses; grace and truth came through Jesus Christ.
JOHN 1:17

The Road Least Traveled
. . . . .

The most radical part of the new covenant was Jesus' inclusive vision of community, which transcended all the prejudices of Hebrew society. Jesus' new community was defined by its focus on doing the will of God, not by the boundaries of bloodlines, geography, politics, or economics. Jesus welcomed every human being into the clan of the chosen people.

No one would be excluded from Jesus' community based on gender, race, creed, socioeconomic status, health, citizenship, or anything else that divides people.

Not even sexual preference?

For example, the twelve apostles were drawn from such humble occupations as fisherman—they were not learned religious leaders. Some of Jesus' closest friends and disciples were women, which was highly unusual for the time. He spent considerable time with those considered sinners and outcasts, such as tax collectors. He was not afraid of lepers or others with communicable diseases. He interacted with other people held in contempt by the Hebrews, including Romans, Samaritans, and Syro-Phoenicians.

Why was Jesus so loving to all kinds of people? At that time, his attitude was even more shocking than it is today.

Opposite: The first light of dawn appears on a hillside of saguaro cactus.

Jesus' new vision of community sprang from a heightened level of consciousness. The four gospels reveal how highly conscious he was.

Love does no harm to its neighbor.
Therefore love is the fulfillment of the law.
PAUL, ROMANS 13:10

The Gospel of Matthew shows that he was committed to Hebrew religious traditions (occipital activity).

The Gospel of Mark, the only gospel probably written by an eyewitness to Jesus' ministry, shows that Jesus was results oriented and often on the go, traveling and performing hands-on work (parietal activity).

The Gospel of Luke emphasizes Jesus' compassionate side (temporal activity).

The Gospel of John reveals the intellectual and mystical dimensions of Jesus (frontal activity).

Cosmic consciousness occurs when someone's cortex is firing equally on all four lobes.

In part, Jesus was able to access a higher level of consciousness because he knew how to love himself, and balance the needs of his mind, body, and soul. All four gospels portray Jesus as someone who walked frequently, spent plenty of time outdoors, and enjoyed food and wine but was not preoccupied with them. His ministry was intellectually challenging and required extensive social interaction. However, no matter how busy he was or how much others expected from him, he made time to be quietly by himself in Nature for reflection and prayer.

Jesus made the time to sit alone quietly. Is our work more important than his was?

During his short ministry, Jesus did everything he could to stimulate the consciousness and spirituality of those around him. He knew that God wants everyone to share this gift, not just a few privileged ones.

Although Jesus was never patronizing to others, he made God's will easy for everyone to understand, regardless of their intelligence or education. No one had to be an expert in the law—the guidelines he gave were simple enough for a child to understand, because he knew that simplicity facilitates consciousness.

First, there is only one God, and he made you for a special reason.

Second, God loves you, and wants you to love her back with everything you've got—heart, soul, mind, strength.

Third, if you love God, love what he has made, starting with yourself.

Fourth, God wants you to treat others as you want to be treated.

Fifth, God is right here with us, so you never have to feel alone or afraid of the dark.

Sixth, God forgives you when you sin, as long as you forgive others and keep trying not to sin.

Seventh, God gets lonely when you ignore her, so talk to her every day—and listen to her, too.

Jesus' most famous technique for sharpening the human mind was telling a parable, a story that relates a spiritual truth. Typically, when someone asked him a question, Jesus would answer with a parable so that the inquirer could discern the truth rather than receive a pat answer. He knew that the parable would cause the listener's conscious mind to focus its attention, and encourage both sides of the cortex to work together (the left focuses on the story's details, the right focuses on the story's meaning).

Ultimately, Jesus called his followers to form a loving community that would obey God's will, expand consciousness, and bring peace to the Earth. Only then will people feel at home and spiritually secure in this life. Only then will the universe be a friendly place.

> *Give ear, O my people, to my teaching;*
> *incline your ears to the words of my mouth.*
> *I will open my mouth in a parable;*
> *I will utter dark sayings from of old,*
> *things that we have heard and known,*
> *that our ancestors have told us.*
> PSALM 78:1-3

The purpose of a civilized human community is to facilitate individual consciousness and spiritual survival.

Jesus knew that his followers would face great difficulties in continuing to build this new-covenant community. To encourage them, Jesus promised to be with them, no matter what, in Matthew 28:20:

And remember, I am with you always, to the end of the age.

After Jesus' death, the Holy Spirit came to help his followers become more conscious and try to live in peace—just as Jesus had promised in John 14:25–26:

For where two or three are gathered in my name, I am there among them.

JESUS, MATTHEW 18:20

I have said these things to you while I am still with you. But the Helper, the Holy Spirit, whom the Father will send in my name, will teach you everything, and remind you of all I have said to you.

Through the teachings of Moses, the prophets, and Jesus, it is clear that the Holy Spirit will see to it that human consciousness evolves—despite all appearances to the contrary. It's only a question of who will choose to reap the kingdom's spiritual harvest in the fields of consciousness.

This is the only reality show that really matters—"Who Wants to Be a Human Being?"

The Road Most Traveled
. . . . .

I believe that men are generally still a little afraid of the dark, though the witches are all hung, and Christianity and candles have been introduced.

HENRY DAVID THOREAU, *Walden*

Since the fifteenth century, expansive new horizons for civilization have opened thanks to discoveries in medicine, science, and technology. Nevertheless, the twentieth century was the most violent yet, as more people died in wars than in all the previous centuries of civilization combined. And the twenty-first century has not gotten off to an encouraging start. Wars and rumors of wars seem to be part of daily life more than ever before.

With civilization's amazing progress over the past five thousand years and the expansion of human consciousness, how can it be that we have remained stuck on the road most traveled—the road that leads to oppression, anxiety, despair, violence, war, and soul-ache?

How can the universe become a friendly place if we can't be friendly to one another?

Every war is supposed to make a country, or the world, a safer, freer, better place. So why haven't ten thousand years of warfare made the world a better place than

Opposite: Auspicious growing conditions attract clusters of saguaro cactus.

it is? Why do billions of people in the world—even in America, the wealthiest nation in history—lack the basics of survival, such as food, clothing, and shelter, not to mention the basics of civilization, such as health care, education, and employment?

Violence and terrorism will never predecease starvation, illiteracy, and boredom.

The land itself is crying out for justice—as its own blood is being spilled. The land of the free is not even free to be land.

Hear, O America: God, the land, and the people are one.

Intellectual abilities and mammalian instincts have brought civilization down the road most traveled—right to the edge of the cliff. Which course will we choose: self-annihilation or cosmic collaboration? We now have the power to realize either outcome almost overnight.

Imagine the number of soultrinos that over six billion people could attract!

As a new millennium begins, the truth is slowly dawning on us: we are waiting for Godot. Institutions obsessed with social power and material wealth—whether they are scientific, political, academic, cultural, religious, or charitable—will never save the day and lead us off the road most traveled.

"For I know the plans I have for you," declares the Lord, "plans to prosper you and not to harm you, plans to give you hope and a future. Then you will call upon me, and I will listen to you."

JEREMIAH 29:11–12

What can we do to escape from the road most traveled—before it's too late?

Here in civilization's greatest experiment ever, we know what to do. It's time to conduct an investigation.

Fortunately, this is something we are good at. As a nation, we excel in audits and investigations of all sorts. From celebrity peccadilloes to airplane crashes, corporate fraud to murders, Ponzi schemes to presidential misconduct, we want to know what happened and try to set things right.

No one topples their own idols better than Americans.

History and our American instincts teach us that we cannot look to our institutions to lead us in this investigation. We need to become proficient at a new type of investigation: self-investigation. The real thing, not navel gazing.

This time, it's personal.

We already have all we need to help one another escape from the road most traveled.

What we need is not around us, but within us—in the Desert wilderness of the human heart.

The human heart—the soul's ambassador to reality and consciousness.

. . . . .

They shall arise in the States,
They shall report Nature, laws, physiology, and happiness,
They shall illustrate Democracy and the kosmos,
They shall be alimentive, amative, perceptive,
They shall be complete men and women.
WALT WHITMAN, *"From Noon to Starry Night: Mediums"*

SIX

Returning

"You will seek me and find me when you seek me with all your heart. I will be found by you," declares the Lord, "and will bring you back from captivity."
JEREMIAH 29:13–14

Watch out! Be on your guard against all kinds of greed; a man's life does not consist in the abundance of his possessions. . . . For where your treasure is, there your heart will be also.
JESUS, LUKE 12:15, 34

Here I am! I stand at the door and knock. If anyone hears my voice and opens the door, I will come in and eat with him, and he with me.
GOD, REVELATION 3:20

I know of no more encouraging fact than the unquestionable ability of man to elevate his life by a conscious endeavor.
HENRY DAVID THOREAU, *Walden*

Opposite: The great horned owl, a top predator in the
Sonoran Desert, patiently roosts while scouting for prey.

One sweltering afternoon in July, there was a rabbit at the water bowl out front. Not that this was unusual, as rabbits are frequent visitors all year long.

But this rabbit was different. One of her ears was neatly sliced off about halfway up.

What misfortune had caused this disfigurement? A birth defect or a close call with a predator? Her ear was quite even across the top, and it didn't appear to be bloody or bothersome. Whatever had happened, it had been a clean job.

Rabbits are typically difficult to tell apart, and this makes it difficult to form any sense of relationship with individual ones. But with this rabbit it was easy. So I named her Ear and a Half. She seemed more gentle and cautious than other rabbits, perhaps to compensate for her extra vulnerability. Perhaps her hearing wasn't optimal.

Most sightings of Ear and a Half occurred at the water bowl or in the side yard west of our house, where a few of her favorite plants lived. One autumn morning I saw her methodically eat up the purple blossoms dropped by a sage plant, working as efficiently as any gardener.

Late one afternoon the following January, I saw Ear and a Half when she was taking one last sip before bedtime. Afterward she hopped a few paces to settle in under a nearby bush along the garage wall. The nights had recently turned cold for the Desert, dropping into the low thirties, and there was a light wind, so this sheltered spot must have felt relatively cozy to her.

That was the last time I saw Ear and a Half. While it is tempting to imagine that she froze to death, the odds are that she was eaten by a predator—especially given what happened the following December.

Early that December, the plentiful population of rabbits in our vicinity went missing in action. And later that month a strange night visitor became the leading suspect.

Late one night a bizarre, otherworldly noise emanated from our roof. It sounded like a teenager yelling for help. I realized that this same creature had paid a nocturnal visit two months earlier, but had quickly flown away when I went to the window.

This time I had a better line of sight and the visitor didn't see me at first. But finally he flew away, and when he did there was no doubt about it: the profile and the wingspan confirmed that he was some type of owl. As if to validate my observation, I immediately heard the sound of a great horned owl claiming the territory with the usual hooooo-hoo-hoo chant.

As I later found out, the strange sound the owl had made earlier was a secondary call of the great horned owl called the harnk, the functions of which are still unclear.

Rabbits are but one of the many creatures that the great horned owl preys upon. With all the noise these owls make, it's hard to imagine that they could catch a rabbit. But their supersensitive hearing and fierce talons give them an edge: they are top predators not only here in the Desert but also throughout the United States.

I am like a desert owl,
like an owl among the ruins.
I lie awake; I have become
like a bird alone on a roof.
PSALM 102:6–7

Maybe rabbits are more appealing to owls come December and January, when several types of accipiters and falcons tend to show up for the dating scene and compete for smaller prey, such as rodents and ground squirrels. Fortunately rabbits hide well and have a lot of fun while they are alive, so their numbers rebound very quickly.

An intense struggle for survival underlies the Desert's calm exterior. Usually it is the vitality of the survivors that gives the Desert her voice. But every now and then, death draws a little closer for a visit and also chimes in.

Life is more like wrestling than dancing, in that it should stand
ready and firm to meet onsets, however unexpected.
MARCUS AURELIUS, *Meditations*

The Dying Tree
. . . . .

One beautiful evening in early May, near sundown I was driving to a class and running a little late. Suddenly a rabbit appeared at the side of the road, obviously startled by my noisy approach on the quiet road.

If he had started across the road a second earlier and I had been driving a bit more slowly, there would have been time to brake and everything would have been fine. Instead there was a sickening, solid thud.

In the rearview mirror, I saw an adult rabbit doing somersaults in my wake, fur flying. No way he could have survived that. And I was late.

Then I remembered all the stunned birds and rabbits we had come upon and had moved from the middle of the road to a safe place over the past few years. Could I do any less this time, when I had been the cause of the accident? So I turned around, parked, and got out, taking a sweater with me.

Surprisingly, the rabbit was alive, lying in the road. There appeared to be no blood, wounds, or broken parts. He was even vigorous enough to struggle and squirm as I wrapped him in the sweater and carried him to a spot protected by tall grasses under a mesquite tree.

He was warm and vital. Once I placed him under the brush, he was quite calm, and I couldn't resist gently stroking him—his long, velvety ears, the rust-colored spot behind his head and shoulders, the soft taupe-colored fur of his bony back and haunches. I knew better than to do this, but I did it anyway, as I told him how pretty he was, and how sorry I was for hurting him, and that everything would be OK.

Off I went to my class, late but confident that the wrong had been righted, and that the rabbit would live.

The next day, I wondered how the rabbit was doing. I stopped to check on him, remembering the place because of the tree. The spot where I had laid him was empty. No carcass and no remains, I was glad to see. Then, nearby in a little trench covered with tall weeds, an unusual color caught my eye: it was a patch of rust-colored fur. I looked closer, and my heart sank as I saw the rabbit lying there.

I looked more closely to see if he was still alive, wondering if he had been lying there suffering for the sixteen hours since the accident. Maybe I should have taken him to an animal rescue center—maybe I still could. My heart was hopeful when I saw a black eye looking shiny and moist, suggesting that he was alive. But on

Opposite: Ocotillo limbs grasp at the remains of the day as the winter sun disappears behind Black Mountain.

I will ransom them from the power of the grave;

I will redeem them from death.

Where, O death, are your plagues?

Where, O grave, is your destruction?

GOD, HOSEA 13:14

closer inspection, I saw that his eye glistened because of countless ants, their industrious bodies forming a seething mass that reflected the sunlight.

Most likely, the rabbit had sustained internal injuries that were not immediately apparent when I helped him. He had probably maintained consciousness long enough to crawl farther away from the road into a hidden spot, where the inner hemorrhaging slowly ended his life.

Had the ants waited until he was dead, or at least unconscious, to begin their work?

Of course not. Why would they? How could they?

As I stood there looking at the rabbit, wondering about what had happened, I had a sense of guilt and remorse for my role, along with a sense of revulsion. But two thoughts soon turned these emotions back.

The first was that these disgusting ants were diligently fulfilling their purpose in life—to clean up the messes left behind by other Desert residents. They were bringing the rabbit back home to the Desert in a new form.

Thank God for ants.

The second thought was that perhaps the rabbit had died a peaceful death, knowing from the rescue attempt and my gentle strokes that some other being cared for him and meant him no harm, despite his misfortune.

Almost every day I pass by the old mesquite tree where I laid the rabbit—the Dying Tree, as I have since named it. I think of that gentle rabbit, unable to comprehend the car and the accident, yet humbly crawling further into the brush to bleed to death and succumb to Nature's demands without complaint.

At least I had told the rabbit the truth: everything would be OK.

Everything was OK. Everything is OK. Everything will be OK.

Our fear of suffering and death makes it hard for us to understand that.

Yet our fear of suffering and death is the only way to begin to understand that.

Because our fear of suffering and death gives us access to the only known cure for unhappiness and soul-ache: the spiritual paradigm shift.

A cure that has worked successfully for over three thousand years.

I say, beware of all enterprises that require new clothes, and not
rather a new wearer of clothes. If there is not a new man, how can
the new clothes be made to fit?

HENRY DAVID THOREAU, *Walden*

In everyday language, the concept of a paradigm shift is pervasive. Many common expressions allude to a significant change in perspective, such as *achieve a break-through, experience a quantum leap, turn over a new leaf, mend one's ways, get real,* and *get a life.*

The term *paradigm shift* became a household word after Thomas Kuhn published *The Structure of Scientific Revolutions* in 1962. In this seminal work, Kuhn described how scientific communities experience relatively quiet periods of "normal science" with minimal innovation, as well as revolutions in scientific thinking that result in the replacement of one paradigm with another—a paradigm shift.

Kuhn explained that the word *paradigm* typically means an accepted model or pattern that is shared by the members of a community. However, his usage of the term had a somewhat different meaning. He compared a scientific paradigm to an accepted judicial decision in common law, in that it is continually being reevaluated under new or more stringent conditions.

In other words, for Kuhn a paradigm was a moving target rather than a fixed one—it was born to change.

Nevertheless, Kuhn found that the change in a community's frame of reference called a paradigm shift occurred gradually and infrequently in science. Calm, stable periods of normal science were needed to examine and understand a paradigm. During these periods, inconsistencies that arose in the accepted paradigm provided opportunities for exploration.

At times, new theories or discoveries by an individual within the scientific community triggered a crisis of confidence in the accepted wisdom. These periods of transition between paradigms were marked by great innovation and numerous competing approaches to address the problems raised by the crisis.

Individuals trigger paradigm shifts—communities and institutions resist them.

For example, the findings of Copernicus, Newton, Lavoisier, and Einstein all created crises that marked the beginnings of revolutions in scientific thought. Each of these scientists relied heavily on the prior findings of others. Einstein cited the work of Galileo, Newton, Maxwell, and Lorentz as the foundations for his findings on relativity.

Communal beliefs and traditions are the launching pad of paradigm shifts.

According to Kuhn, a crisis indicated that a good opportunity for retooling the community's paradigm had arrived—just as a crisis in business might cause a company to retool its factory. However, in times of crisis there was a danger that no paradigm would be accepted. Kuhn warned that to reject an old paradigm before a new one had been embraced is to reject science itself.

Kuhn found that scientific progress takes place through a messy, nonlinear combination of prior findings, experience, anomalies, and new theories. Yet most scientific textbooks erroneously portrayed scientific history as a neat, linear progression of findings.

Even though scientific communities are in many ways unique, Kuhn noted that his findings have some applicability to other fields of endeavor.

Indeed, the concepts that underlie Kuhn's description of a paradigm shift in scientific thinking are helpful in understanding the concept of *metanoia*—Greek for "beyond knowing"—which conveys a change of heart, or a spiritual paradigm shift.

A Change of Heart

| *The unexamined life is not worth living to a human.*
| SOCRATES

. . . . .

For over three thousand years, *metanoia* has been helping individuals deal with crises and become more conscious—since long before anyone knew that the Earth revolves around the sun.

A paradigm shift or *metanoia* sounds like a great idea—as long as someone else

Opposite: Selflessly parting with stored moisture, a saguaro blooms profusely in response to the crisis of drought.

Everything comes from you, and we have given you only what comes from your hand.

DAVID TO GOD,
1 CHRONICLES 29:14

is going through it. Most individuals vigorously resist a paradigm shift and the uncertainty associated with it. They tend to stumble into one, rather than seek it out. New ideas can shatter well-loved delusions, as when everyone finally realized that the emperor had no clothes in the familiar children's story.

Metanoia *chases self-destructive dark energy out of the heart.*

Amid the routines and challenges of daily life, it is difficult to change priorities, attitudes, and behavior. However, a crisis tends to heighten conscious attention to what's going on around and within a person. It brings awareness that existing coping methods might need some adjustment.

Our moulting season, like that of the fowls, must be a crisis in our lives.
HENRY DAVID THOREAU, *Walden*

Crisis wakes up consciousness.

A desire to end the psychic and even physical discomfort triggered by crisis opens the mind to new possibilities and solutions. For example, a divorce, heart attack, or layoff can lead to a change of heart that introduces beneficial lifestyle changes.

In other words, crisis and *metanoia* work together to expand consciousness. They slough off the dull layers of the mind created by ignorance, ruts, and delusions.

Crisis and metanoia. *The dynamic duo.*

While the term *metanoia* may not be as familiar as *paradigm shift,* the process of experiencing a change of heart about someone or something is naturally fascinating to us. From the Bible to the literary classics of Western civilization to the sappy love stories and grisly homicide tales of today, stories of *metanoia* have intrigued people for over three thousand years.

We're hard-wired to go beyond knowing.

Partly because they combine both images and sound, movies have been a powerful medium for the portrayal of *metanoia.* Such popular film classics as *Gone with the Wind, Casablanca, Psycho, The Birds, Dr. Zhivago,* and *The Sound of Music* all tell stories involving *metanoia.*

However, to illustrate how crisis and *metanoia* can help us become more conscious, there's no better story than the one about Ebeneezer Scrooge.

Repentance is a kind of self-reproof for having neglected something useful; for that which is good is something useful, and the good man's object in life.
MARCUS AURELIUS, *Meditations*

A memorable portrayal of *metanoia* as a profound spiritual experience is the 1953 movie classic *Scrooge,* starring Alastair Sim as Ebeneezer Scrooge, the famous old fool we love to hate.

Based on the novel *A Christmas Carol,* written by Charles Dickens in 1844 and set in London at the dawn of the industrial age, this tale is really not so much about Christmas as about how the human heart is transformed by *metanoia.* The following comments are based on the book, which the movie follows more or less faithfully.

Scrooge was introduced as a wealthy older man, clearly unhappy and hostile toward everything and everyone, including himself. He was exceptionally fond of making money—and he was good at it.

One Christmas Eve, the ghost of his departed longtime partner Jacob Marley paid Scrooge a visit to let him know that things were not going well in the afterlife. Marley, bound in chains, regretted that he had lost forever the ability to help others:

"Why did I walk through crowds of fellow-beings with my eyes turned down, and never raise them to that blessed Star which led the Wise Men to a poor abode? Were there no poor homes to which its light would have conducted *me?*"

When Scrooge tried to console him by pointing out that he had always been a good man of business, Marley shook his chains loudly and screamed in agony:

"Business! Mankind was my business. The common welfare was my business; charity, mercy, forbearance, and benevolence were my business. The dealings of my trade were but a drop in the water in the comprehensive ocean of my business!"

In order to save Scrooge from this fate, Marley arranged for three spirits to visit Scrooge, despite his protests: the Ghosts of Christmas Past, Christmas Present, and Christmas Future. These spirits helped Scrooge to conduct a thorough investigation of his entire life—how he had spent his time, what he had accomplished, and how his life would end.

From the Ghost of Christmas Past we learn that Scrooge had handled life's difficulties well as a boy and a young man, until his beloved sister died. In his grief, he hid his vulnerable heart behind an obsession with wealth and power.

Whoever loves money never has money enough; whoever loves wealth is never satisfied with his income. This too is meaningless.
ECCLESIASTES 5:10

Psychic pain invites our mammalian instincts to run wild and suffocate soultrinos.

The ghost revealed that when Scrooge was a young man, his girlfriend had broken off their relationship, observing how he had changed his worldview:

> "You fear the world too much," she answered gently. "All your other hopes have merged into the hope of being beyond the chance of its sordid reproach. I have seen your nobler aspirations fall off one by one, until the master passion, Gain, engrosses you."

Scrooge had a paradigm shrink—the opposite of metanoia.

In several scenes, the Ghost of Christmas Present showed Scrooge that the few people currently in his life either despised him or felt sorry for him. As they watched Scrooge's clerk Bob Cratchit celebrating Christmas with his large family, Scrooge's heart was moved with compassion for sweet Tiny Tim, Bob's crippled son.

When Scrooge asked the ghost if Tiny Tim would live, the ghost repeated back Scrooge's own harsh words from an earlier time—if he's inclined to die, let him go ahead and do so, and decrease the population. As Scrooge expressed concern about Tiny Tim's fate, the ghost reprimanded him for his attitude toward others:

> "Will you decide what men shall live, and what men shall die? It may be in the sight of Heaven you are more worthless and less fit to live than millions like this poor man's child. O God! to hear the insect on the leaf pronouncing on the too much life among his hungry brothers in the dust!"

Even so, Scrooge was unwilling to change his greedy, heartless behavior until a crisis occurred. The eerie Ghost of Christmas Future made death personal for Scrooge and destroyed his self-delusions. The ghost showed Scrooge that his wealth would not protect him from the world's sordid reproach after all—others would use his death as an opportunity to carry off his beloved possessions. For Scrooge the future held a disgraceful, ignominious death. He would be mourned by no one.

It's the relationships, stupid.

Galvanized by this grim portrait, Scrooge finally accepted that he had a choice in the matter. He experienced a profound *metanoia* and decided to change his life's course. He awakened on Christmas morning a new man, joyfully determined to use his wealth to help other people. The next day, Cratchit was shocked when Scrooge declared he was going to raise his salary. Scrooge assured him that he hadn't lost his senses, but had in fact come to them.

> *The best repentance is to up and act for righteousness, and forget that you ever had any relations with sin.*
> WILLIAM JAMES,
> *The Varieties of Religious Experience*

In the course of the story, Scrooge changed from controlling, arrogant, and annoying to joyful, humble, and helpful. As he moved beyond fear and greed, his mission in life changed from accumulating wealth to helping others. He returned to being in right relationship with God, the Creation, others, and self.

Metanoia *happens when human somethingness embraces divine otherness.*

Scrooge teaches us that expanding consciousness and improving relationships go hand in hand. Once *metanoia* enabled Scrooge to transform his need to control life into a willingness to enjoy life, he was able to treat himself and others more compassionately.

Just as a return to the senses precedes *metanoia,* a change in outlook and behavior always follows true *metanoia,* because a new person emerges from the experience.

Like a form of spiritual aerobics, *metanoia* brings an increase in the volume of life flowing through the spiritual heart—which needs exercise as desperately as the physical heart.

No one can serve

two masters. Either

he will hate the one

and love the other, or

he will be devoted to

the one and despise

the other. You cannot

serve both God

and Money.

JESUS, MATTHEW 6:24

Metanoia *infuses the heart with soultrinos—the lifeblood of the living God.*

We often talk about something coming from the heart or about having a change of heart. But do we know what the "heart" is?

Do we change our own hearts, or is the change brought about by an act of God?

Is crisis a prerequisite to *metanoia,* or is there an easier way to achieve it?

Can we learn to tell when a crisis is coming the way a saguaro can?

Dickens's fable is of little help on these issues. We have to do a little time traveling ourselves to get a better understanding of the heart and how it functions.

We have to go back to the Middle Eastern Desert of some three thousand years ago, to the earliest protégés of *metanoia:* the Hebrew prophets.

I will give you a new heart and put a new spirit in you; I will remove from you your heart of stone and give you a heart of flesh. And I will put my Spirit in you and move you to follow my decrees and be careful to keep my laws.

GOD, EZEKIEL 36:26–27

The Messengers of God
. . . . .

The ancient Hebrews had a holistic view of a human being. They saw the self as an integrated entity of mind, body, soul, heart, and spirit. They believed there was no way to isolate these parts, yet they figured that each played a different role in a person's life.

They considered the heart a facet of the self unique to humans, an invisible nexus of beliefs, experiences, thoughts, feelings, and personality where decisions for action are made, and where compassion, morality, and willfulness are seated.

The heart is where consciousness lives.

As we saw previously, a central focus of Hebrew worship was this command from Deuteronomy 6:5 to love God deeply with the heart and soul:

You shall love the Lord your God with all your heart, and with all your soul, and with all your might.

Opposite: Despite similar growing conditions, these saguaros have experienced different outcomes in their struggle for survival.

Yet this command was difficult to follow, despite the Hebrews' best intentions. They would sin, or miss the mark, and fall out of right relationship with God, the Creation, others, and self. Someone who had fallen out of right relationship with God was said to have a proud or hard heart.

Some individuals played a special role in pointing out the Hebrews' lapses in maintaining right relationship (righteousness) with God. The prophets believed that God had given them a message through visions or dreams to deliver to God's people. By sharing these messages, they tried to bring *metanoia* and righteousness to Hebrew society.

By your wisdom and understanding you have gained wealth for yourself and amassed gold and silver in your treasuries.
By your great skill in trading you have increased your wealth, and because of your wealth your heart has grown proud.
EZEKIEL 28:4–5

These messengers of God played a crucial role in the Hebrews' spiritual and political lives for over eight hundred years, beginning around 1100 BC. Unlike the Hebrew religious leaders, they were equally concerned with the letter of the law *and* the spirit of the law.

Often the prophets crossed all social and economic boundaries, holding the rich and powerful Hebrews accountable for their idolatry and exploitation of society's most vulnerable members, including widows, orphans, the impoverished, and foreigners.

Those endowed with wealth and power should have been the most conscious members of society—and the most compassionate. They were the ones who should have shown gratitude to God for their good fortune by helping others rather than grasping for even more wealth.

They sound like Ebeneezer Scrooge.

The prophets' message was unwelcome to the elite—which is probably why the prophets were often mistreated and even murdered.

There were several distinct groups of prophets. Over three thousand years ago, the earliest prophets, such as Samuel, Nathan, Elijah, and Elisha, advised the first kings of Israel after the monarchy was established by Saul in 1050 BC.

They were the earliest accountability partners.

After the successful yet corrupt reign of Solomon ended in the tenth century BC, amid economic and religious squabbles, the Hebrew kingdom divided into two parts—the northern kingdom of Israel and the southern kingdom of Judah.

During the eighth century BC, Hebrew society in both kingdoms was riddled with corruption and spiritual decadence—idolatry, sorcery, and even child sacrifice. During these times, a second prominent group of prophets arose: Amos and Hosea from Israel, and Isaiah and Micah from Judah.

The eighth-century Hebrew prophets' emphasis on *metanoia* and social justice was distinctive, an early sign of the worldwide surge in consciousness that culminated in the sixth century BC and witnessed the lives of Zoroaster (630–553 BC), Lao-tse (604–531 BC), Confucius (551–479 BC), and Buddha (550–480 BC), as well as the advent of classical Greek civilization.

The latter prophets, such as Jeremiah and Ezekiel, prophesied around the tempestuous sixth century BC, when the Babylonian Empire ruled the Middle East. In 587 BC, the Babylonians retaliated against Judah for an unsuccessful rebellion and forced many Hebrews, especially their leaders, into exile in Babylon.

After the Hebrews returned from exile in 538 BC, another generation of prophets, including Haggai and Zechariah, counseled them. The last of this prophetic line was probably Malachai, who lived about four hundred years before Jesus was born.

In hindsight, the Hebrews might have avoided many crises by heeding the warnings of the prophets and changing their selfish ways. But they didn't listen.

We are a lot like them.

Not even when the master of *metanoia* himself spoke: Isaiah, son of Amoz, who predicted the arrival of a messiah who would bring justice to Hebrew society.

> *The heart is deceitful above all things*
> *and beyond cure.*
> *Who can understand it?*
> *"I the Lord search the heart and examine*
> *the mind,*
> *to reward a man according to his conduct,*
> *according to what his deeds deserve."*
> JEREMIAH 17:9–10

Returning to the Senses

. . . . .

They will beat their swords into plowshares and their spears
into pruning hooks.
Nation will not take up sword against nation, nor will they train
for war anymore.
Come, O house of Jacob, let us walk in the light of the Lord.

ISAIAH 2:4–5

One of the most prominent of the Hebrew prophets was Isaiah, who lived in Jerusalem (located in Judah) from 740 to 680 BC. Unlike most of the prophets, he was a wealthy, well-educated poet and politician—one of the elite's own, widely respected despite his unpopular message.

In a remarkable passage, Isaiah described how he had voluntarily become a prophet in response to God's call during a vision he had at the temple. God wanted Isaiah to urge the Hebrews to seek *metanoia,* as indicated in Isaiah 6:8–10:

> Then I heard the voice of the Lord saying, "Whom shall I send? And who
>   will go for us?"
> And I said, "Here am I. Send me!"
> He said, "Go and tell this people:
> 'You will be ever hearing, but never understanding;
> you will be ever seeing, but never perceiving.'
> Make the heart of this people calloused;
> make their ears dull
> and close their eyes.
> Otherwise they might see with their eyes,
> hear with their ears,
> understand with their hearts,
> and turn and be healed."

This passage is difficult to understand, but a few things seem clear. It affirms that the heart has senses that aid in understanding spiritual reality, just as the

Opposite: After generous spring rains, a prickly pear cactus eaten to a stump by javelinas sprouts numerous new pads.

*A shoot will come up
from the stump of Jesse;
from his roots a Branch
will bear fruit. . . .
He will not judge by
what he sees with his eyes,
or decide by what he
hears with his ears;
but with righteousness
he will judge the needy,
with justice he will give
decisions for the poor
of the earth.*

ISAIAH 11:1–4

body's senses help in interpreting physical reality. Somehow, understanding with the heart, turning toward God, and healing are inextricably linked.

Metanoia *helps us return to the senses of our hearts.*

God does not force service or *metanoia* on anyone, but politely asks and waits for a response. But why did God instruct Isaiah to dull the Hebrews' hearts? It sounds as if God did not want the Hebrews to turn and be healed—and be conscious. More likely, this was another portrayal of God as having human feelings—God is using sarcasm, much as people do when frustrated with others' misdeeds.

OK, be that way then!

Isaiah called God "The Holy One of Israel," and wrote extensively about the divine perspective and concerns. A major theme in Isaiah's writings is the political oppression and economic exploitation of the less privileged members of Hebrew society, as expressed in Isaiah 1:16–17:

> Stop doing wrong,
> learn to do right!
> Seek justice,
> encourage the oppressed.
> Defend the cause of the fatherless,
> plead the case of the widow.

Isaiah's time was rife with political uncertainty. The Hebrew kingdom of Israel joined Syria to attack the Hebrew kingdom of Judah in 735 BC. A powerful neighbor, the Assyrian Empire, conquered the kingdom of Israel in 722 BC and vanquished its identity as a nation. Political unrest simmered in Judah.

"What do you mean by crushing my people and grinding the faces of the poor?" declares the Lord, the Lord Almighty.

ISAIAH 3:15

Has anything changed in the Middle East since then?

In both kingdoms, Hebrew leaders were preoccupied with keeping their enemies at bay and ignored social justice in their own society. They refused to admit that the behavior they feared in others—political oppression and economic exploitation—was the same behavior they displayed in the daily affairs of Hebrew society.

Despite the suffering, corruption, and political instability around him, Isaiah envisioned the unfolding of a very different world that God was determined to bring about. He predicted that a remnant of Israel descended from Jesse, the father of David, would survive and produce a new spiritual leader with a fully functioning heart—a leader who would obey God and show compassion for all.

This expansive vision encompassed not only all human beings, but also the whole Creation. According to Isaiah, some day predation, shame, suffering, death, and war would no longer dominate the Earth—justice and peace would prevail.

In an unprecedented way, Isaiah described this new world using several different metaphors, including the holy mountain of God, as indicated in this passage from Isaiah 11:6–9:

> The wolf shall live with the lamb
> the leopard shall lie down with the kid,
> the calf and the lion and the fatling together,
> and a little child shall lead them. . . .
> They will not hurt or destroy on all my holy mountain;
> For the earth will be full of the knowledge of the Lord
> as the waters cover the sea.

Isaiah urged his fellow Hebrews to obey God's will for fairness and peace in their society, and to become a spiritual light to the nations. He warned them that if they did not change their ways, Hebrew society would come to ruin, and their temple would be destroyed by foreigners.

But the Hebrews didn't listen and change their ways. They waited for a crisis rather than heeding the warnings of Isaiah and the other eighth-century prophets. Indeed, Jerusalem fell and the temple was destroyed for the first time in 587 BC, about a hundred years after Isaiah died.

Of all the Hebrew prophets, Isaiah had the most universal message. He is quoted more often in the New Testament than all of the other prophets combined.

He was the obvious favorite of the greatest teacher of *metanoia* the world has ever known: Jesus of Nazareth.

In the Desert
· · · · ·

Do not think that I have come to abolish the Law or the Prophets; I have not come to abolish them but to fulfill them.

JESUS, MATTHEW 5:17

We have very little information about the birth, the childhood, and much of the adulthood of Jesus. The Gospels of Mark and John have nothing at all to say about these periods of his life. However, the Gospels of Matthew, Mark, Luke, and John all agree on the events that launched Jesus' three-year ministry of healing, preaching, and teaching when he was about thirty years old.

All four gospels indicate that a Hebrew known as John the Baptist was living out in the Judean Desert, quoting Isaiah 40:3 and baptizing people. They relate how John the Baptist announced that the messiah would be coming, and that Jesus went to the Jordan River and was baptized by John.

The so-called synoptic gospels of Matthew, Mark, and Luke (those that appear to share a similar source) also mention that John the Baptist was calling people to repent of their sins. They report that, shortly after his baptism, Jesus was "led by the Spirit" into the Desert.

Led by the Spirit.

What was that experience like for Jesus?—An inkling? A suggestion? An idea? A thought? A feeling? A brainstorm?

What did it sound like?—A bell ringing? A voice calling? A rustling in the leaves? A thunderstorm?

What did it feel like?—An impulse? The sun on his face? A breeze in his hair? A slap on his head? A child pulling on his hand? A lover's kiss? A soul-ache in his chest?

Why did the Spirit lead Jesus into the Desert? Was it because of what was there—the sun, the moon, the stars, the Earth, and the Desert? Or perhaps what was not there was what mattered. The Desert's sparseness encourages the mind to reject clutter and human ways, and embrace contemplation and Nature's ways.

Opposite: This major wash in the Anza-Borrego Desert State Park of California is a conduit for both storm runoff and recreation.

A voice of one calling
in the desert:
"Prepare the way
for the Lord;
make straight in
the wilderness
a highway for our God."

ISAIAH 40:3

Most likely, the Spirit led Jesus into the Desert to find the life that is truly life. Amid the threats of deprivation and death in the Desert, life becomes even more precious to the heart.

The Desert's hostility makes the soul yearn for God's friendliness.

The synoptic gospels recount that Jesus remained in the Desert and fasted for forty days. Mark 1:13 tells us that Jesus was not alone:

> He was with the wild animals, and the angels attended him.

What was Jesus thinking? What was happening to his brain chemistry?

During this sojourn, the Gospels of Matthew and Luke tell us that Satan (the devil) tempted Jesus in three specific ways. Each time, Jesus responded to Satan with a short quote from Moses rather than relying on his own words.

When Satan suggested that Jesus turn stones into bread if he was the Son of God, Luke 4:4 relates that Jesus quoted Deuteronomy 8:3:

> It is written: Man does not live by bread alone, but on every word that comes from the mouth of God.

The devil has a huge ego and knows how to toy with the human ego.

When Satan told Jesus that he would give him all the kingdoms and wealth in the world, which were his to give, if Jesus would worship him, Luke 4:8 reveals that Jesus responded with Deuteronomy 6:13:

> It is written: Worship the Lord your God and serve him only.

The devil is a wealthy, selfish control freak with an insatiable appetite for power.

When Satan led Jesus to the highest point of the temple in Jerusalem and suggested that he throw himself off it, because it is written in Psalm 91:11–12 that God will send angels to rescue those who dwell with him, Luke 4:12 confirms that Jesus answered with Deuteronomy 6:16:

> It says: Do not put the Lord your God to the test.

Satan likes to play mind games to lead us toward self-destruction.

This was a battle of wits rather than one involving physical violence—and the territory they were fighting over was nothing less than Jesus' very heart and soul.

At the end of this time of trial, according to Luke 4:13, Satan conceded the battle, but not the war:

When the devil had finished all this tempting, he left him until an opportune time.

Satan is lazy, looking for an easy mark and a moment of vulnerability.

So how did Jesus triumph over Satan's clever tricks in the Desert?

Jesus conquered Satan with the wisdom of his spiritual traditions and the power of love.

Knowing that he was vulnerable to Satan's wiles and delusion, Jesus did not rely on his own thoughts during his time of trial—he relied on his memory. He stood his ground spiritually by grasping onto the tried and true wisdom of Moses from his spiritual traditions.

As a result, Jesus was able to overpower Satan by loving him enough to forgive him for his rebellion against God. He felt sorry for him and loved him, just as he did people that were beholden to Satan (for example, the rich man in Mark 10:17–22). He just said no to Satan. He even found polite, instructive ways to say no to Satan, rather than ridiculing, hurting, or destroying him.

If we forgive Satan for rebelling, we can no longer withhold forgiveness from others and ourselves.

This record of Jesus' Desert sojourn affirms that Satan and God both want us, but for very different reasons—and we have the freedom to choose our master. If we choose an idol, something other than God, Satan always slips in the back door like the thief that he is.

Idols are made out of matter—animals, people, buildings, cars, or money.

The Spirit led Jesus into the Desert to experience *metanoia* and make sure he was mentally and spiritually prepared to help others. After Jesus overcame the temptations of worldly rewards, egotism, and idolatry in the Desert, his consciousness took a quantum leap.

Once Jesus left the Desert, he immediately began to prove how fully conscious he was by sharing the good news with everyone around him.

Does Satan serve God by bringing crisis into our lives to force conscious choices?

Get a Life

. . . . .

Then Peter came to Jesus and asked, "Lord, how many times shall I forgive my brother when he sins against me? Up to seven times?" Jesus answered, "I tell you, not seven times, but seventy times seven times."
MATTHEW 18:21–22

After this period of temptation in the Desert, the Gospels of Matthew and Mark tell us that Jesus went into Galilee with this message, quoted from Mark 1:15:

The time has come. The kingdom of God is near. Repent and believe the good news!

From the original Greek of the four gospels, various forms of the word *metanoia* are often translated into English as *repent* and *repentance*. Although the definition of repent is "to turn from sin and dedicate oneself to the amendment of one's life," the word is often associated with guilt. However, the gospels used *metanoia* to convey a sense of turning away with the mind—more similar to what we mean today by the term *paradigm shift*.

Something got lost in the translation.

Jesus' message was not one of gloom and doom, damnation and punishment. His message was full of joy and excitement! Jesus' experience in the Desert transformed his frame of reference. For him, God's kingdom, heaven, was a friendly place, and it was not "out there" or "up there" somewhere. He told everyone that it's right here, right now, receivable through the senses of the heart.

The senses are four-dimensional—mind, body, heart, and soul.

If Jesus were preaching today, he might say something like this: "Something really sweet is happening. The waves of the Divine Dimension are running through us right here, right now. It's a good thing. Get a life, and be a part of it! And don't be fooled by Satan. He's been living off his inheritance, spending even the principal—and it's almost all gone, so he wants what you have. Just say no to him and you're home free."

Satan is the original cheater cell. By his own choice, he consumes matter, energy, and souls in a selfish manner without any concern for others, as a tumor consumes nourishment. He can only destroy life. He cannot create it or help it grow.

The soul will be filled with either Satan's dark energy or soultrinos—it's up to us.

Fortunately, Satan's control is limited to worldly things, like food, clothing, shelter, status, money, and power.

Worldly wealth, in and of itself, is not a bad thing. In Luke 16:9, Jesus indicates that it can be of great advantage to one who uses it to enhance human relationships:

> *What good is it for a man to gain the whole world, and yet lose or forfeit his very self?*
>
> JESUS, LUKE 9:25

I tell you, use worldly wealth to gain friends for
yourselves, so that when it is gone, you will be welcomed into eternal dwellings.

However, Satan skillfully distracts the heart with worldly wealth, and then stakes a claim on the soul. *Metanoia* is the main defense we have against the seductive lies and delusions spun by Satan, which disrupt consciousness and lead us to fear, greed, violence, and soul-ache.

Metanoia *tames our inner reptile and inner mammal.*

What are the fruits of *metanoia?* How does God know when we have had a change of heart?

John the Baptist shared some very specific ideas on this topic. After he warned the Hebrews about the coming wrath of God, they asked him what they should do. This passage from Luke 3:11–14 indicates that honesty, humility, and service are the new types of behavior that *metanoia* brings:

John answered, "The man with two tunics should share with him who has none,
and the one who has food should do the same."
Tax collectors also came to be baptized. "Teacher," they asked, "What should we do?"
"Don't collect any more than you are required to," he told them.
Then some soldiers asked him, "And what should we do?"
He replied, "Don't extort money and don't accuse people falsely—be content with
your pay."

Jesus' most important teaching on *metanoia* is contained in the parable of the prodigal son, found only in the Gospel of Luke (15:11–32). In this story, Jesus explained how love, forgiveness, and joy are the most important fruits of *metanoia.*

After depleting his inheritance, the prodigal son experienced *metanoia* amid desperation and crisis. When the son returned home, the father had compassion on him and ran out to meet him. Obviously, the father had forgiven his son before he even knew he had repented. However, the father called for a celebration only *after* the son acknowledged his sins.

Like the father in the parable, God yearns for all of us to return home willingly through *metanoia*. God's love and forgiveness are always there waiting for us, whether we deserve them or not. *Metanoia* does not earn these divine gifts—it allows us to *feel* them. *Metanoia* enables us to escape guilt and feel loved and forgiven, so that we can be loving and forgiving to others.

"Let's have a feast and celebrate. For this son of mine was dead and is alive again; he was lost and is found." So they began to celebrate.
JESUS, LUKE 16:25

Open the door to higher consciousness with a loving heart.

In this story, Jesus said it twice so we couldn't miss it: the father was overjoyed that his "bad boy" had come home. However, the mean-spirited older brother resented the father's joy and celebration over his younger brother's return.

Based on this parable, we know what's really going on in the universe. God created everything—so God created Satan. God gave Satan the freedom to rebel, and Satan used his inheritance unwisely just like the prodigal son. Just like the father, God wants his bad boy Satan to come home. God does not want us to act like the older brother, resisting the joyful reunion of his family.

God will decide if anything or anyone in the Creation is not redeemable. It is not for us to condemn parts of God's handiwork—including Satan or other people. God's love and forgiveness heal the brokenness of the universe, and lead us home to divine harmony.

Collaboration exists in the universe because of God's forgiving love for all.

Opposite: A barrel cactus produces abundant fruit after summer rains.

Bear fruits worthy
of repentance.

<small>JOHN THE BAPTIST,</small>
<small>LUKE 3:8</small>

The Cosmic Battle
· · · · ·

*Throw away vain hopes and come to your own aid, while yet you may,
if you care at all for yourself.*
MARCUS AURELIUS, *Meditations*

Through the teachings of Moses, the prophets, and Jesus, all human beings have received a spiritual heritage that transcends all religions and human institutions. Could Jews own Moses or Isaiah, or could Christians own Jesus?

This inheritance reveals that we have our hands full, spiritually speaking. The human heart is the main battleground for the conflict between the cosmic forces of self-destruction and collaboration. Led by Satan, our natural instincts and emotions keep seducing us back onto the road most traveled—the road of anxiety, despair, and violence.

Our main line of defense against this spiritual poison is *metanoia,* which helps us to stay in right relationship with God, the Creation, others, and self.

Institutions don't have hearts—they rely on the hearts of individuals. Institutions cannot experience *metanoia* and lead the way to higher consciousness—only individuals can do that.

Only individuals can care enough to address the problems that America faces today, these for starters:

44 million people are uninsured (including many children)
10 million are illegal immigrants (including many children)
9 million people are unemployed (including many parents)
4 million people are homeless (including many children)

There are a lot of Tiny Tims here in America—let alone the rest of the world.
Are we giving God a soul-ache?

Which individuals are in the best position to address such pervasive problems? The people like Scrooge—the wealthy. It's not their money that's needed as much as their know-how about how to get things done in this world. They have the political clout to focus our institutions on solving the right problems. They are worth so much more than their money.

Those who have more should be the most conscious—and the most helpful.

America has less than 5 percent of the global population, yet almost half of the world's billionaires and a good portion of its millionaires. But what good is all this wealth if civilization as we know it ends?

Ask the Hohokam.

It is not only enlightened self-interest that should motivate the wealthy—it is gratitude.

Anyone with even a speck of humility will tell you that his or her financial success was not fully attributable to personal smarts, family connections, or hard work. In every story, a special factor plays a central role. Some call it good timing—being in the right place at the right time. Others call it opportunity, coincidence, or luck. A few call it help. Even fewer call it the grace of God.

> *From everyone who has been given much, much will be demanded; and from the one who has been entrusted with much, much more will be asked.*
> JESUS, LUKE 12:48

Only God knows if anyone truly deserves to be wealthy or poor.

Through some combination of worldly experiences, relationships, personal crisis, and grace, every human being is given the opportunity to learn that the cosmos is ruled by a friendly power greater than one's self. This friendly power is politely yet persistently knocking at every heart's front door every day, waiting to be invited in.

After fourteen billion years of waiting, God must be glad that we're finally here.

God is up to something—and we have work to do.

. . . . .

And I saw quite clearly how much God is pleased when a person comes to him in all simplicity, as it were quite naked, unafraid and trusting.
LADY JULIAN OF NORWICH, *Revelation of Love*

SEVEN

Harmony

And they reported to the angel of the Lord, who was standing among the myrtle trees, "We have gone throughout the earth and found the whole world at rest and in peace."

ZECHARIAH 1:11

Therefore I tell you, whatever you ask for in prayer, believe that you have received it, and it will be yours. And when you stand praying, if you hold anything against anyone, forgive him, so that your Father in heaven may forgive you your sins.

JESUS, MARK 11:25

Likewise the Spirit helps us in our weakness; for we do not know how to pray as we ought, but that very Spirit intercedes with sighs too deep for words.

PAUL, ROMANS 8:26 NRSV

We and God have business with each other; and in opening ourselves to his influence our deepest destiny is fulfilled.

WILLIAM JAMES, *The Varieties of Religious Experience*

Opposite: Like identical twins, these two saguaros have grown from the same roots.

*M*any people around the world know the saguaro, a familiar symbol of the American Southwest. If you are near a saguaro, chances are you are in the Sonoran Desert, the only place in the world where this cactus grows.

Ranging up to sixty feet tall, these charismatic giants have a friendly look, with their arms reaching up as if to wave or praise. They are always ready to welcome us when we return home—no matter where we've been.

In addition to the saguaro, the other Sonoran native that really makes this Desert feel like home is the Gambel's quail. More like a terrestrial animal than a bird, Gambel's quail prefer to walk on the ground rather than to fly, a habit that makes them vulnerable to speeding cars but easier to observe than other birds.

They are highly sociable, living in families with up to twenty-four members. They frequently call to one another to express affection, concern, excitement, and annoyance. Sometimes they just seem to reassure each other with a clear pattern of call and response: "Where are you?" "Here I am."

Despite an innate tendency toward water conservation, quail are common visitors to the water bowl in the front of our house. With their outlandish costumes that seem overly opulent for this harsh environment, families come to the bowl and then leave it like groups of trick-or-treaters scurrying about on Halloween.

As I learned the hard way, quail like to introduce their chicks to the water bowl routine as soon as they are hatched.

One July morning, I happened to look out the kitchen window, and there was a dark object in the water bowl. Unfortunately, a baby quail less than one week old was floating on the surface. Although the water was only about two inches deep, once she became wet, the youngster had been unable to escape with her flimsy wings.

I seize the descending man and raise him
with resistless will,
O despairer, here is my neck,
By God, you shall not go down!
Hang your whole weight upon me.
WALT WHITMAN, *"Song of Myself"*

I took the hapless youngster out of the water and gently pressed her chest with my thumb several times. Water bubbled out of her nose and mouth and, much to my surprise, she began to come around. Quickly I set her down several feet from the water bowl, confident that her folks would be back for her, as quail are extremely diligent about gathering the lost members of their flock.

Watching from inside the house, I saw that the little quail's first attempts to walk were not promising. She appeared to have brain damage from the accident. Like a tiny drunk, she stumbled around with uncontrolled movements.

She made her way to the end of the sidewalk and stood in the hot morning sunshine trying to recover. Up the driveway came a handsome quail couple to visit the water bowl. They approached the chick, realized that something was wrong with her, and started to peck at her as if to suggest that this little reject shouldn't even think about joining them.

I will search for the lost and bring back the strays. I will bind up the injured and strengthen the weak . . . I will shepherd the flock with justice.

God, Ezekiel 34:16

Although saddened by this cruelty, I refrained from "rescuing" the chick because it had been only ten minutes since I had pulled her from the water. Birds have an amazing ability to recover from an accident if they survive, so I thought I would give the chick and her parents more time to reunite.

As I had suspected, the chick made a full recovery. Within twenty minutes of her rescue, she was moving around as if nothing had happened. Her instinct told her to stay right at the spot where she had last seen her parents.

She jumped up into the branches of a stubby sage nearby as if to get a better vantage point, just as adult quail do when they are on the lookout. I began to think that it was time to catch her and take her to an animal rescue center, as it seemed that her parents had left her for dead.

Just before I left the window, the chick scurried across the driveway and into the Desert. I immediately went to look for her, but never saw her again. It's as if she knew my thoughts and decided she would rather take her chances in the Desert, where she belongs.

At least several rocks added to the bottom of the water bowl prevented a recurrence of the incident.

I wonder if the poor little quail ever found her family, or if she became a tasty snack for a snake or coyote. Either way, the Desert's harmony was served.

How can true harmony include abandonment and predation?

Several weeks ago, another quail chick became separated from her clan along the driveway. A little older than the other chick, this youngster was able to fly up to a tall ocotillo branch—a favorite quail perch. She repeatedly wailed the juvenile distress signal. Sure enough, Papa responded to her cry for help within a minute. He reunited the chick with the nearby clan as Mama watched and clucked with concern.

The living God is always there to answer our cry for help and bring us home.

Above: Gambel's quail are a common sight year round. This male is alert for predators as he watches over his family.

Despite the Desert's difficult living conditions, Gambel's quail and many other creatures are obviously quite at home here. Even the youngsters skillfully handle the threats and opportunities of daily life.

But when these Desert dwellers are out of their element, it's a very different story.

> *I believe that in every little thing created by God there is more than we realize, even in so small a thing as a tiny ant.*
> TERESA OF AVILA, *The Interior Castle*

when wings Get Wet
. . . . .

Anyone who has ever visited the Salt River Valley or flown overhead knows that swimming pools abound here, despite the Desert's legacy of drought. Pools are commonly found in the yards of both older and newer homes.

These days, most people here don't think much about water, as long as it's clean and comes running when called. Some people have filled in their pools out of concern for water usage. A few who maintain pools conserve water in other ways to keep their consumption moderate. Until taps run dry, pools will no doubt continue to flourish in this broiling land of rock and sun.

This is good news for the animals, as they seem to enjoy the pools far more than people do.

However, this modern version of the watering hole is a mixed blessing for the Desert's creatures. Like Lorelei singing to sailors along the Rhine, a pool seduces every sort of critter with its refreshing offer of a drink or a snack of shipwrecked insects.

Like the siren's song, the pool proves to be more a death trap than an oasis. Sometimes Desert animals end up dead in the pool, probably never having suspected that a quick bite, sip, or dip would lead to their demise.

> *The mass of men lead lives of quiet desperation. What is called resignation is confirmed desperation.*
> HENRY DAVID THOREAU, *Walden*

However, nothing goes to waste in the Desert. Every day a coyote, vulture, or crow comes around to check the spot we have designated for carcasses.

Daily the opportunity arrives to help a living creature that's struggling to escape a watery grave—although most victims seem more horrified than pleased by the rescue attempt.

Comfortable in the water, red-spotted toads cannot resist jumping into the pool, but they cannot always jump out from the spot where the floating filter hose is located. On several occasions, a stranded red-spotted toad has required a helping hand. Several times an adult female and a juvenile (I assume mother and child, but who knows with amphibians?) have been stranded together, and the exhausted junior has sat atop Mama's back as they've awaited their fate.

Snakes occasionally slither over for a graceful poolside drink, but rarely get stuck in the pool. Yet one day a beautiful red racer who swam quite well needed a lift out of the water.

Lizards periodically get trapped in the water, even the little babies. They are almost indestructible. One day we saw a six-inch adult lizard lying on the bottom of the pool. We almost left him for dead, but something told me to fish him out. I put him on the deck in the sun and gently pressed his back several times. Sure enough, the seemingly dead lizard came back to life before our very eyes, and eventually scampered off into the Desert.

One morning there was a live baby mouse on the filter hose and an adult dead in the pool, suggesting that they had ventured out on the hose together before Mom fell off and drowned.

However, the vast majority of the time, the hapless victim to be rescued from the pool is an arthropod. This makes sense, since arthropods represent over 85 percent of the animal species living on the Earth today. Yet it seems that arthropods should know better, given that they have been around for over four hundred million years and have endured five mass extinctions.

For years it never even occurred to me to rescue an arthropod from the pool. Bugs and spiders—yuck! "Who cares?" I thought. But then one day I saw a tarantula floating in the pool, apparently dead. The thought of inspecting the fierce-looking spider up close and personal intrigued me. Much to my surprise, he started to move as soon as the net I extended got near him.

Rejoice with me, for this spider of ours was dead and is alive again; he was lost and is found.

I rescued him and admired his furry, velvety brown and black body. Then I watched as he crawled back into the Desert's protective brush, where he obviously felt at home.

Ever since, I have been an equal-opportunity rescuer. Why should a mammal, bird, reptile, or amphibian have more of a right to live than an arthropod? If anything, arthropods are more deserving of rescue, given their leading role in the food chain.

For why will you die, O house of Arthropod? I take pleasure in the death of no one.

My efforts have been amply rewarded. Arthropods have taught me many things—first and foremost, to keep trying. Help might arrive at any moment. Even the tiniest bug floundering on the surface of the water makes a noticeable ring of ripples, making his plight conspicuous and giving the rescuer a sense of urgency.

God sees a struggle within the heart the way we see a bug's ring on the water.

If at all possible, arthropods latch onto something in the pool—a feather, a leaf, a blossom, other bugs, the filter hose, the chlorine float, or anything at all that can help them get out of the water. The socially minded ants latch onto one another and form a little raft—all for one and one for all to the very end.

Whatever they cling to, arthropods hang on with all their might as they wait to die—or perhaps get eaten. With the precision of assassins, the Say's phoebes, lesser nighthawks, and bats swoop down and take what they want, like vultures around a carcass.

Regardless of appearances, if a shipwrecked arthropod is helped out of a pool, usually there's hope; many survive even if they've been motionless for a long time.

O happy living things! no tongue
Their beauty might declare;
A spring of love gushed from my heart,
And I blessed them unaware,—
Sure my kind saint took pity on me
And I blessed them unaware.
The selfsame moment I could pray;
And from my neck so free
The albatross fell off, and sank
Like lead into the sea.
SAMUEL TAYLOR COLERIDGE,
"Rime of the Ancient Mariner"

However, a would-be rescuer can do more harm than good. A careless rescue attempt could easily maim or kill, since arthropods are fragile when wet. It is one thing to pull an arthropod out of the pool; it is another thing to give her a future with hope.

Once a winged arthropod is safely out of the pool, he goes through a painstaking routine to make sure all his tiny parts are dry and ready for flight, just as any pilot would. The way a winged arthropod starts revving up before takeoff is reminiscent of an airplane on the runway.

It's thrilling to see an arthropod seemingly come back from the dead to resume her journey toward fulfilling whatever purpose she was created for—probably pollinating flowers and thus saving other species from extinction, rather than dying in a swimming pool.

If an arthropod's life has meaning, how can a human life be without purpose?

Of all the animals I've rescued from the pool, only one has been smart enough to recognize help when it appears: the honeybee. If she has any energy left, the honeybee will fearlessly abandon whatever floating refuge she has sought and jump back into the water to swim toward a proffered net, obviously confident in the net's ability to save her life.

This clever insect is not native to the Sonoran Desert, but was introduced from Europe for beekeeping purposes long ago and eventually got loose. In the wetter climes where the species originally evolved, perhaps the honeybee developed the instinct to realize its vulnerability once its wings get wet.

It is a shame when the soul is first to give way in this life, and the body does not give way.
MARCUS AURELIUS, *Meditations*

How is it that a honeybee instinctively knows the difference between a temporary fix and a lasting solution, and we don't when we are spiritually shipwrecked? We cling to illusion, delusion, neurosis, obsession, and addiction like bugs trapped in a pool, refusing to let go and take hold of the liberating net that God extends to us.

We need to become more conscious to gain the sense of a honeybee.

Until evolution delivers this instinct to our species genetically, we must develop

our own techniques to recognize the difference between the "help" that keeps us trapped and the help that can truly save us.

The first step in doing this is to know when we are in trouble.

That's easy. Every moment of our lives, we are either in trouble or headed for it, seduced by the siren's song of worldly delights sung by our mammalian instincts.

The second step is to see the net and swim toward it.

That's the hard part.

Above: Although it is not a native, the honeybee is a common pollinator in the Sonoran Desert.

The Higher Power
. . . . .

> *Since the sense of Presence of a higher and friendly power seems to be the fundamental feature of the spiritual life, I will begin with that. . . . Apart from anything acutely religious, we all have moments when the universal life seems to wrap us round with friendliness.*
>
> WILLIAM JAMES, *The Varieties of Religious Experience*

Spiritually, we are in the world but not of the world—we are out of our element, just like Desert creatures trapped in a swimming pool. The discomfort caused by this spiritual friction makes us do something uniquely human: our hearts cry for help, as if someone can hear us.

For many thousands of years, human communities have sought help from a higher power in the pursuit of life, liberty, and happiness amid Nature's cruel indifference. We call this search for spiritual help religion. The word *religion* comes from the Latin word meaning "to bind together," signifying the bond between humanity and the divine.

> *I believe in you my soul, the other I am must not abase itself to you And you must not be abased to the other.*
>
> WALT WHITMAN, *"Song of Myself"*

Soultrinos seal the bond between humanity and the divine.

At the end of the nineteenth century, William James was a Harvard professor and a leading pioneer in exploring the psychology of religion. Ultimately he concluded that all religion begins with a cry for help, and that the benefits of personal religious experiences were the same for everyone, regardless of their religion.

In 1902 James published his seminal work *The Varieties of Religious Experience.* While he admitted that the word *religion* is difficult to define, he provided this definition for his own use of the term:

> Religion . . . shall mean for us *the feelings, acts, and experiences of individual men in their solitude, so far as they apprehend themselves to stand in relation to whatever they may consider the divine.*

James found that all creeds address a human being's uneasiness at having two parts of the self—a wrong part and a higher part:

1. The uneasiness, reduced to its simplest terms, is the sense that there is *something wrong about us* as we naturally stand.
2. The solution is the sense that we are *saved from the wrongness* by making proper connection with the higher powers.

Once an individual identifies his or her real being with the friendly higher power, similar feelings occur regardless of the person's religious tradition. James cited emotional states involving a loss of worry and the experience of humility, joy, security, happiness, tenderness, charity, peace, and harmony. These uniquely human feelings arise from a whole new outlook on life called the faith-state, which results from the person's relationship with the higher power:

> He becomes conscious that this higher part is coterminous and continuous with a *more* of the same quality, which is operative in the universe outside of him, and which he can keep in working touch with, and in a fashion get on board of and save himself when all his lower being has gone to pieces in the wreck.

Faith. The divine answer to humanity's cry for help.

Even though these feelings elude plenty of religious people, James suggested that the expansive emotional dimension of the faith-state moves far beyond morality and is the distinguishing feature of religion:

> If religion is to mean anything definite for us, it seems to me that we ought to take it as meaning this added dimension of emotion. . . . It ought to mean nothing short of this new reach of freedom for us, with the struggle over, the keynote of the universe sounding in our ears, and everlasting possession spread before our eyes. This sort of happiness in the absolute and everlasting is what we find nowhere but in religion.

Nevertheless, despite the sense of elation there is work to be done in the faith-state. When someone in this state achieves prayerful communion with the higher power, higher energies flow into the unconscious mind and bring healing and other positive results into the world. James described the results of these incursions into the mind:

> At these places at least, I say, it would seem as though transmundane energies, God, if you will, produced immediate effects within the natural world to which the rest of our experience belongs.

God, Nature, soultrinos, and the unconscious mind can lead the world toward healing and peace.

For most of human history, this faith-state was associated with the experience of natural phenomena rather than with facts. Although modern faith has a much higher intellectual content than ever before, James believed that religion alone can produce real experiences. Science provides only intellectual experiences. Reality lies in our experience with natural phenomena, and thus religious experience aids us in staying in touch with reality:

> It does not follow, because our ancestors made so many errors of fact and mixed them up with their religion, that we should therefore leave off being religious at all. By being religious we establish ourselves in possession of ultimate reality at the only points at which reality is given us to guard.

The living God is in the experience of phenomena—not in the study of phenomena.

Faith in something is a requirement of human existence. The absence of faith (*anhedonia*) brings physical distress and death. James cited the potent combination of faith-states and creeds as one of the most important biological functions of mankind.

The fool says in his heart, "There is no God."
DAVID, PSALM 14:1

Faith and soultrinos interact in four dimensions: mind, body, heart, and soul.

Because of his expertise in psychology, James even speculated on the psychological mechanism that might be at work in producing the faith-state's new outlook on life:

Let me then propose, as an hypothesis, that whatever it may be on the *farther* side, the "more" with which in religious experience we feel ourselves connected is on its *hither* side the subconscious continuation of our conscious life.

Ultimately James reached a very practical conclusion as to the true purpose of religion in daily affairs—achievement of a better life:

Does God really exist? How does he exist? What is he? are so many irrelevant questions. Not God, but life, more life, a larger, richer, more satisfying life is, in the last analysis, the end of religion. . . . God is real because he produces real effects.

Even though James's findings are over a hundred years old, they are even more relevant today, in light of current thinking on how the human mind works. The uniquely human feelings associated with the faith-state arise from a healthy, stable mind that can maintain consciousness.

Civilization fails when consciousness and faith fail.

Cerebral wealth, not financial wealth, is the key to overcoming fear and having faith in a friendly higher power. It is also the key to promoting the peaceful co-existence of religions today—so we can all cry for help in our own way.

All parts of the universe are interwoven with one another, and the bond is sacred. Nothing is unconnected with some other thing. MARCUS AURELIUS, *Meditations*	## The New Age · · · · ·

Today about 75 percent of the world's population adheres to one of four major religions: Christianity (33 percent), Islam (22 percent), Hinduism (15 percent), and Buddhism (6 percent). Judaism, one of the world's oldest religions and the foundation for Christianity and Islam, is the religion of less than one-half of 1 percent of the world's population. The rest of the global population either adheres to a variety of other religions (10 percent) or declares itself unaffiliated or atheistic (14 percent).

If William James was correct about the common spiritual ground shared by all

The desert and the parched land will be glad;

the wilderness will rejoice and blossom.

Like the crocus, it will burst into bloom;

it will rejoice greatly and shout for joy.

Isaiah 35:1–2

religions, this is not obvious based on the past and present violence in the world that is linked to religious differences. Yet it is not faith but the secondary expressions of religion—creeds, philosophies, and theologies—that make religion an instrument of violence.

The dark energy of self-destruction loves to hide behind the mask of religion.

The common spiritual basis of all religions is evident when personal religious freedom flourishes owing to a strong separation of religion and state. Such freedom has traditionally existed in America—God's Own Country, as W. Somerset Maugham called it in his 1933 novel *The Razor's Edge.*

As a political entity, America has always had an experimental personality. Not surprisingly, America has been just as adventurous in her approach to spirituality and religion.

Religion, American style. Truer than the red, white, and blue.

Have whatever religion you want. Have your religion with or without God, Christ, Satan, the Bible, rules, faith, sex, compassion, justice, community, worship, or spirituality. Have your religion in person or on television—or even on the Internet. If a religion hasn't already been established that is to your liking, make up your own.

Have it your way. But where's the beef?

Religion, American style, comes with or without just about anything—except for one common

> *He has told you, O mortal, what is good; and what does God require of you but to do justice, and love kindness, and to walk humbly with your God?*
> Micah 6:8

element. From the beginning, American-style religion has been inseparable from great spiritual awakenings—group forms of *metanoia* equivalent to vast spiritual high-pressure systems.

Awakenings that cause consciousness to burn all the brighter in large groups of people.

Opposite: The Desert has played a major role in the development of several world religions, including Judaism, Christianity, and Islam.

Awakenings that tip the cosmos toward harmony.

Awakenings that will continue until the world ends.

Over the past three hundred years, America has experienced several major spiritual awakenings, each coinciding with an important chapter in American history. Each awakening has echoed the call to consciousness of the Old Testament prophets and the gospels more than the dictates of any particular religious creed.

Examples include the First Great Awakening of eighteenth-century colonial America, the Second Great Awakening that occurred on the frontier in the early to mid-1800s, the abolitionist movement leading up to the Civil War, and the social gospel movement in industrial America at the end of the nineteenth century.

You ain't seen nothing yet.

Today the great American spiritual awakening called the New Age is in full swing—but it's not quite what we think it is. It has little to do with Aquarius, goddesses, crystals, feng shui, Wicca, magic, or aliens.

Rather, the New Age is about spiritual righteousness colliding with the physical universe. This is the New Age of Right Relationship—and of putting universal spiritual values ahead of everything that divides people, including religious affiliations, political agendas, and economic concerns.

Blessed are those who hunger and thirst for righteousness, for they will be filled. . . . Blessed are those who are persecuted because of righteousness, for theirs is the kingdom of heaven.
JESUS, MATTHEW 5:6, 10

The New Age is the eternal truth born anew in the current space and time.

Easily understood from children, Nature, and the Bible, these universal spiritual values are the basis for maintaining right relationship with the higher power and all divine phenomena: one's self, other human beings, the web of life, the Earth, and the cosmos.

A yearning for right relationship keeps the heart's door open for God.

In a giant spiritual leap forward for humanity, the New Age brings together the ancient wisdom of Genesis and Einstein's theory of relativity: both human beings and the universe around them are defined by their relationships. And the New Age also includes the view of God that Jesus gave us: God is our loving parent, not our hostile judge.

This New Age awakening is a global phenomenon. It has been in the works for a hundred years, sprouting amid the unprecedented violence and spiritual hurricanes of the twentieth century. However, its rumblings have been most evident in America.

As Europe endured decades of political hostilities, war, and revolution in the twentieth century, the New Age was pushing through American soil. Relationships among society, government, individuals, and the environment were being challenged and redefined in unprecedented ways.

> *The conservation of natural resources is the fundamental problem. Unless we solve that problem it will avail us little to solve all others.*
>
> THEODORE ROOSEVELT

In hindsight, it is not difficult to see milestones that provide evidence of this new growth:

1902–1909—President Theodore Roosevelt preserves over 230 million acres of federal land.

1910—Americans popularize the concept of the "week-end" for the first time in history.

1920—American women receive the legal right to vote as Tennessee ratifies the Nineteenth Amendment.

1925—The Scopes Monkey Trial in Dayton, Tennessee, affirms the separation of religion and state.

1935—President Franklin Roosevelt signs the Social Security Act to provide a financial safety net for all Americans.

1935—Alcoholics Anonymous forms in New York, eventually introducing the Twelve Steps to addiction recovery based on universal spiritual values.

1946—American leadership and Allied collaboration in World War II lead to an international alliance named the United Nations with permanent headquarters in New York.

1954—The United States Supreme Court declares segregation unconstitution-
al, leading to the birth of an ecumenical civil rights movement.

1967—The National Guard shoots four young protesters at Kent State
University amid an antiwar movement that includes demonstrations and
draft evasion on an unprecedented scale.

These events were just a few of the early signs of a new spiritual awakening. The New Age was irrevocably launched by the disillusionment and alienation engendered by John F. Kennedy's assassination, the Vietnam War's senseless casualties, and the Watergate scandal—all within a ten-year period.

We hold these truths to be self-evident: all men are created equal, and are endowed by their creator with the right to life, liberty, and the pursuit of happiness.
THE UNITED STATES
DECLARATION OF INDEPENDENCE

This New Age of Right Relationship has galvanized many Americans to reconsider the meaning of the phrase "all men are created equal." For our founding fathers, "all men" meant all white Christian men who owned land.

In addition, the New Age leads Americans to address the questions "Who is my neighbor?" and "How do I love my neighbor as myself?" within the context of universal spiritual values that transcend religious dogma and creeds. Children, Nature, the Bible, Twelve-Step programs, and small groups are the nurturers of spiritual growth in the New Age.

If children are our spiritual advisers, why are there so many Tiny Tims?

The New Age is forcing Americans to examine many relationships in a whole new way.

What does it mean to be in right relationship with what God has created?

What does it mean to be in right relationship with one's self—mind, body, heart, soul, and spirit?

What does it mean to be in right relationship with other people and other species?

Opposite: A wash begins to run after a late summer storm.

I hate, I despise your religious feasts;

I cannot stand your assemblies. . . .

Away with the noise of your songs!

I will not listen to the music of your harps.

But let justice roll on like a river,

righteousness like a never-failing stream!

GOD, AMOS 5:21, 23–24

What does it mean for believers to be in right relationship with those of other faiths and nonbelievers?

What does it mean for institutional leaders to be in right relationship with their constituents?

What does it mean for the wealthiest country in the world to be in right relationship with other nations—and the Earth?

Justice is love in action, transforming all that is not love into love.

If anyone considers himself religious and yet does not keep a tight rein on his tongue, he deceives himself and his religion is worthless.

JAMES 1:26

America has pushed the battle over right relationship out of the halls of power and into the "streets" of everyday life—right where it belongs. Even American movies, music, books, talk shows, reality shows, and cartoons are peppered with issues of right relationship.

And now, there's no turning back. Because of the expansion of consciousness wrought by the New Age, Americans will no longer follow those who do not lead, even if they are priests, physicians, professors, politicians, or presidents.

Those who lead us to self-destruction are not leaders.

Because of the New Age, a new and improved American Dream is America's top export, rather than pornography, entertainment, consumer brands, environmental degradation, weapons, corporate hegemony, or political arrogance.

Despite the materialism and insecurity that dominate the collective American psyche of the early twenty-first century, an ancient, powerful force is behind this latest spiritual eruption from deep within the American heart.

It's the same potent force that first appeared in the Hebrews thousands of years ago: faith in an almighty Creator that is beyond human control and comprehension.

The Desert, consciousness, faith, and God have been partners for almost four thousand years.

Some time later God tested Abraham. He said to him, "Abràham!"
"Here I am," he replied.

GENESIS 22:1

call and
Response
. . . . .

Around four thousand years ago, Abraham began his life as Abram (meaning "exalted father") in the town of Haran. He was descended from a group of people from the town of Ur, which was probably near the mouth of the Euphrates River in today's Iraq. Through their affiliation with Judaism, Christianity, and Islam, over half of the world's people honor Abraham as the first man of faith.

While the term *faith* does not appear before the time of Moses in most Bible translations, the account of Abraham's behavior in Genesis 12–22 reveals a deep faith in God, a degree of faith that was uncommon for one who lived four thousand years ago. His relationship with God was reverent yet friendly, marked by mutual trust, generosity, and challenge.

Unexpectedly, God called an aged, childless Abram to leave his home for an unknown destination. At the time, Abram little suspected that the area where he lived would lie in ruins within two hundred years, after the Sumerian civilization's fertile cropland turned to desert.

Abram and his family became the holy remnant, saved for a latent purpose.

In Genesis 12:2–3, God promised Abram that he would give him great blessings, blessings meant to be shared with others:

I will make you into a great nation and I will bless you;
I will make your name great, and you will be a blessing.
I will bless those who bless you, and curse those who curse you;
And all the people on earth will be blessed through you.

Despite the risks of leaving home for an unknown destination, Abram trusted God and responded positively to God's call. He left his home with his wife Sarai and nephew Lot. An extended sojourn took them through Canaan to Egypt, then back to Canaan.

God and the Desert were making them more conscious.

*If you do not
stand firm in
your faith,
you will not
stand at all.*

Isaiah 7:9

Abram complained to God that a servant would have to be his heir since he was childless. God reassured Abram about the future in Genesis 15:5–6:

> [God] took him outside and said, "Look up at the heavens and count the stars— if indeed you can count them . . . so shall your offspring be." Abram believed the Lord, and he credited it to him as righteousness.

Abram had no visible evidence to support his belief in God's promise. Both he and his wife Sarai were old, and they had never conceived a child. Nevertheless, Abram trusted God and obeyed him, and thus was considered righteous—in right relationship with God.

Righteousness is proof of faith.

Because of Abram's faithful response, God made a covenant with him. And God renamed him Abraham (meaning "father of many") and renamed his wife Sarah. Under the covenant, both God and Abraham (as well as Abraham's descendants) would have responsibilities. According to the Torah, God has always linked possession of the Promised Land to righteousness.

Despite their mutual trust and goodwill, God and Abraham continued to challenge each other. When God informed Abraham that Sodom and Gomorrah were on the divine watch list for obliteration because of their grievous sins, in Genesis 18:23–25 Abraham questioned how God makes decisions:

> What if there are fifty righteous people in the city? Will you really sweep it away and not spare the place for the sake of the fifty righteous people in it? Far be it from you to do such a thing—to kill the righteous with the wicked, treating the righteous and the wicked alike. Far be it from you! Will not the Judge of all the earth do right?

When God answered that he would spare the city for the sake of fifty righteous people, Abraham reverently but persistently bargained with God. Would God

Opposite: A dead saguaro will eventually become unable to support its own weight and will fall over.

spare the city for forty righteous people? For thirty, twenty, or ten? Each time, God responded positively.

God wants to reason with us.

"Come now, let us reason together,"
says the Lord.
ISAIAH 1:18

Later God tested Abraham's faith by asking him to kill his beloved son Isaac as an offering to God. Without protest or complaint, Abraham prepared to obey God's request. At the last minute, God's angel told Abraham not to harm Isaac, and a ram with his horns caught in a bush became the sacrifice.

Abraham responded to God's call of his own free will. God treated Abraham not as a puppet or a slave, but as a partner. This unique relationship with God, embodied by the covenant between them, became the basis for the Hebrews' religion.

Because of his faithfulness, Abraham became the spiritual father of a vast multitude throughout the nations of the world—just as God had promised.

Taste and see that the LORD is good;
blessed is the man who
takes refuge in him.
DAVID, PSALM 34:8

A major theme throughout the Old Testament is that God needs the help of faithful people like Abraham to accomplish the divine agenda in this world. Many Hebrews after Abraham, including Moses, Samuel, David, and Isaiah, followed Abraham's example. They listened to God's call and faithfully responded, willing to obey God. In turn, God helped them and treated them fairly. God was good to them.

Who wants to seek help from a higher power that acts like a dictator or a tyrant?

And it was Abraham's descendant Jesus who showed the world just how powerful faith truly is.

God tastes good to the human soul, and nourishes it completely.

"What do you want me to do for you?" Jesus asked him.
The blind man said, "Rabbi, I want to see."

MARK 10:51

The Power
Surge
· · · · ·

More than anything else, Jesus saw his mission as helping people to relate to the divine presence in their daily lives with faith. Even though the New Testament is much shorter than the Old Testament, the word *faith* appears more than ten times as often in it. Faith is a uniquely human feeling, a product of consciousness.

As this passage from Matthew 23:23–24 indicates, Jesus felt that the Hebrew religious leaders were not setting a good example for others in matters of faith:

> Woe to you, scribes and Pharisees, hypocrites! For you tithe mint, dill, and cum-
> min, and have neglected the weightier matters of the law: justice and mercy and
> faith. It is these that you ought to have practiced without neglecting the others.
> You blind guides! You strain out a gnat but swallow a camel!

Since the religious leaders were not doing a good job of promoting conscious-ness and faith in their society, Jesus spent much of his time doing just that. Some have even speculated that Jesus' original goal was not to start a new religion, but to reform Judaism, making it a religion of the conscious.

In teaching about faith, Jesus emphasized the importance of positive thinking, healing, and nonviolence.

In Luke 8:50, Jesus revealed that the mind can shape its own reality and tran-scend death when connected to God though faith, without the interference of neg-ative emotions such as fear. When told of the death of the young daughter of Jairus, a synagogue official, he said:

> Do not fear. Only believe, and she will be saved.

Jesus' ability to relieve people's suffering was a phenomenal part of his ministry. Faith had to be present in both the healer and the one being healed in order for healing to occur. Even so, he was not quick to take the credit for healing; repeat-edly he told people that their own faith had healed them.

When a hemorrhaging woman secretly touched Jesus from behind, he immediately noticed and asked who had done it. His apostles suggested that it had been the crowd brushing by him. As related in Luke 8:46–48, Jesus knew better:

> But Jesus said, "Someone touched me; for I noticed that power had gone out from me." When the woman came forward and declared she was healed, he said to her, "Daughter, your faith has made you well; go in peace."

Faith feels like physical, mental, and spiritual well-being.

A strong commitment to the health, consciousness, and life of every individual was the foundation of Jesus' most radical teaching—the practice of nonviolence.

The Way
. . . . .

> *Love your enemies and pray for those who persecute you, that you may be sons of your Father in heaven. . . . If you love those who love you, what reward will you get?*
> JESUS, MATTHEW 5:43–46

Jesus is the strongest proponent of nonviolence the world has ever known. Those modern leaders who have used nonviolence successfully, such as Mahatma Gandhi and Martin Luther King Jr., modeled their movements on Jesus' teachings.

In perhaps one of the most controversial passages in the gospels (Luke 6:27–31), Jesus called for a new attitude toward enemies:

> Love your enemies, do good to those that hate you, bless those who curse you, pray for those who mistreat you. If someone strikes you on the cheek, turn to him the other also. If someone takes your cloak, do not stop him from taking your tunic. Give to everyone who asks you, and if anyone takes what belongs to you, do not demand it back. Do to others as you would have them do to you.

Many of Jesus' followers over the past two thousand years have had trouble with this teaching, and have thus ignored it. Why would Jesus want us to be a bunch of wimps or victims? How can we prevail in this world if we follow his advice?

Opposite: A rare snowfall brings welcome moisture to the Pinnacle Peak area of the upper Sonoran Desert.

See, I am doing a new thing!

Now it springs up; do you not perceive it?

I am making a way in the desert

And streams in the wasteland.

GOD, ISAIAH 43:19

Nevertheless, the gospels show how Jesus triumphed over the same worldly problems we face today by using a nonviolent approach.

Nonviolence keeps the dark energy of self-destruction away from the human heart.

Despite all the personal attacks and rejection he experienced during his three-year ministry, never once did Jesus sanction violence. When his disciples proposed a violent response to a village that had rejected Jesus, he had an unequivocal response, as Luke 9:54–56 relates:

> When the disciples James and John saw this, they asked, "Lord, do you want us to call fire down from heaven to destroy them?" But Jesus turned and rebuked them. And he said, "You do not know what kind of spirit you are of, for the Son of Man did not come to destroy men's lives, but to save them."

Even though Jesus was rejected by that village, he was later accepted by many—without recourse to soul-numbing revenge and violence.

Violence is the opposite of righteousness.

Physical violence was not the only kind of violence that Jesus prohibited. In Matthew 5:21–22, he taught that the spiritual violence of having a bad attitude toward another person is a matter no less serious than such acts of physical violence as murder:

> You have heard that it was said to the people long ago, "Do not murder, and anyone who murders is subject to judgment." But I tell you that anyone who is angry with his brother will be subject to judgment. . . . Anyone who says, "You fool!" will be in danger of the fire of hell.

Jesus changed the world through kindness and compassion, not hostility and cruelty. Other people's behavior never justified any form of violence—not even when Jesus' very life was threatened. When the soldiers came to capture him at the Garden of Gethsemane, one of his companions drew his sword and cut off the ear of the high priest's servant. In Matthew 26:52, Jesus told his follower:

> Put your sword back in its place, for all who draw the sword will die by the sword.

Eventually, Jesus was tortured and crucified. Despite this humiliating death,

Jesus won the battle *and* the war. Even while he was dying on the cross, he showed no bitterness. He quoted the psalms to express his feelings and asked God to forgive the ones who had tortured and executed him. He died in a state of right relationship with God, the Creation, others, and himself—and thereby preserved the life of his immortal soul.

Jesus was all that. He's all that still. He'll be all that forever.

When Jesus first saw his disciples after his resurrection, he had no harsh words for them. You'd think he would have been upset with them, but he didn't reproach them for deserting him when he needed them most. In Luke 24:36 and John 19:19 and 19:26, Jesus had these words for his disciples:

Peace be with you.

No possession or victory in this world is more valuable than the human soul. To commit violence is to be at war with God, and to risk losing one's soul forever.

There is no just war for Christians.

However, we are not alone when trouble comes our way. Prayer can help us achieve anything worth achieving in this world. Jesus assured us that God always answers our prayers.

God answers prayer in a way that promotes consciousness, righteousness, and cosmic harmony.

If we love God, we seek God through prayer—just as God seeks us.

If we love our selves and our neighbors, we forgive them—just as God forgives us.

A new command I give you: Love one another. As I have loved you, so you must love one another. By this all men will know that you are my disciples, if you love one another.

JESUS, JOHN 13:34–35

Ultimately, Jesus taught that violence would never bring peace to the soul or to the Earth. The Old Testament's "eye for an eye, tooth for a tooth" approach to life was not in line with God's will. God wants us to love one another, not harm and kill one another—no matter what.

Jesus' message of love, forgiveness, and nonviolence is the way to spiritual security—in this life and the next.

Nonviolence promotes cosmic consciousness.

The universe . . . takes a turn genuinely for the worse or for the better in proportion as each one of us fulfills or evades God's demands.
WILLIAM JAMES, *The Varieties of Religious Experience*

Over the past four thousand years, the Bible's spiritual geniuses and others who came after them have shown us that having healthy, loving relationships with God, the Creation, others, and self is the bottom line of human spirituality. Indeed, the word salvation comes from the Latin word for health.

The human spirit nourishes the mind, body, heart, and soul through healthy relationships.

Because of the universe's self-destructive tendencies, healthy relationships with God, the Creation, others, and self don't just happen—they require a conscious effort. Therefore, the most meaningful work in life is to become increasingly conscious, and help *all* others do the same.

We can save one another from self-destruction—just like we did during the ice age.

Throughout civilization's history, the Desert has been the best whetstone for sharpening human consciousness, because the Desert's harshness forces us to confront the spiritual discomfort that is inherent in the human condition. We are in the world, but not of the world.

In the Desert, abundance can be found only within the soul.

That's what makes the upper Sonoran Desert so special. Because this Desert receives a few more inches of rain than a Desert should, she shows us how scarcity can indeed encounter abundance in this world.

We praise You, Lord, for all Your creatures, especially for Brother Sun, who is the day through whom you give us light.
FRANCIS OF ASSISI, *The Canticle of Brother Sun*

With waving arms, the Sonoran Desert's unique saguaros constantly remind us that the universe truly is a friendly place, as long as we are looking for love in all the right places—in our relationships and not in the physical world.

In bold defiance of Brother Sun's oppressive stare, the saguaros raise their arms with praise and thanksgiving for the blessings of this life—even after they die.

The saguaros are the true freedom fighters of America.

But it's not just this Desert that holds the truth. The whole Creation—Nature and humanity—teaches us that we can feast on the richest of fare here and now, and throughout eternity.

For this Creator lives
With no other thought
Than to love and be loved
By we.

There are no unsolvable problems in this world. It's time to come to our senses and return home.

There is a secret to life, and the Big and Little Dippers have been trying to share it all along. Just as the dippers share the same likeness but not the same size, we human beings have to be content sharing the image of God, but not the divine power and grandeur.

Since Adam and Eve, humans have been trying to grab the Big Dipper out of God's hands. Jesus made it clear that by accepting the more humble Little Dipper and leaving the Big Dipper to God, we can bring health to the body, consciousness to the mind, love to the heart, and peace to the soul.

Soul-ache ends when we allow God to fill our dipper.

Just as Paul taught us almost two thousand years ago, the universal spiritual values that lead us to consciousness and spiritual security are easily discerned from what God has made. Now we know how right he was:

Share like a supernova.	Guard like a reptile.
Reflect like a planet.	Cooperate like a mammal.
Watch like the moon.	Walk like a hominid.
Nourish like the Earth.	Smile like a baby.
Listen like a mountain.	Enjoy like a child.
Simplify like water.	Love like an adult.
Thank like a plant.	Trust like a friend.
Struggle like an arthropod.	Forgive like a child of God.

Amid the chaos of self-destructive collisions in the universe, the living God blends together all opposites and contradictions in an orderly manner. As long as we keep trying to be conscious and keep trying to love God, the Creation, others, and ourselves, we cannot go wrong—despite all appearances to the contrary. Over time, collaboration always trumps self-destruction.

Harmony is chaos viewed from a distance.

Spiritually, we have nothing to fear from the universe. The life that is truly life can never be taken away from us. Our place on the sprital map of the universe is easy to find. We belong where God is.

In eternity there is indeed something true and sublime. But all these times and places and occasions are now and here. God himself culminates in the present moment, and will never be more divine in the lapse of all the ages.
HENRY DAVID THOREAU, *Walden*

And God is right here with us, easily encountered along the razor's edge where somethingness collides with otherness:

Where the negative meets the positive.

Where the unconscious meets the conscious.

Where experience meets understanding.

Where ignorance meets knowledge.

Where oppression meets freedom.

Where suffering meets joy.

Where fear meets faith.

Where violence meets righteousness.

Where death meets life.

Where self-destruction meets collaboration.

After fourteen billion years of partnering with the universe, God has given only one message for all of us. Throughout the entire Creation, the divine message is there to guide us toward collaboration and spiritual security in a self-destructive universe.

Opposite: An agave bloom reaches high into the sky at sunset.

You are right here with me. Keep trying!
Love, God

Epilogue

I have seen you in the sanctuary
and beheld your power and your glory.
Because your love is better than life,
my lips will glorify you.
I will praise you as long as I live,
and in your name I will lift up my hands.
My soul will be satisfied as with the richest of foods;
with singing lips my mouth will praise you.

DAVID, PSALM 63:2–5

MAY THE PEACE OF GOD, WHICH SURPASSES
ALL UNDERSTANDING AND RELIGION,
BE WITH YOU NOW AND FOREVER.

Opposite: A well-nourished saguaro reaches
triumphantly toward the sky despite the sun's harsh glare.

✤ ACKNOWLEDGMENTS ✤

The patient, persistent family members who provided brutally frank comments on my earliest drafts are my uncredited co-authors: Peter Strupp, Walter A. Tysenn, Walter J. Tysenn, and Werner Strupp. Without their early and honest feedback, I could not have written this book. Joyce Ditzler contributed greatly in this regard as well.

My mother Phyllis Tysenn and my friends Nancy Fulcher and Heather Walker encouraged me early and often to keep at it—often when there was seemingly no good reason for doing so.

Having acknowledged the sources of so much personal help, I must also thank those who assisted me professionally. My copyeditor, Marilyn Martin, challenged both my writing and my theology in constructive ways, doggedly helping me to refine my thoughts over many months.

Barbara Jellow, who handled the design, art evaluation, and composition, produced an inspiring vision of the book, one that energized me to push forward during the editing and production process. James Gleason, Andrew Clarke, Peter Ho, Alex Lee, and their colleagues at Asia Pacific Offset/Phoenix Offset were always collaborative and flexible in handling our printing arrangements.

Several publishing professionals gave generously of their time and expertise in helping me navigate the choppy waters that lie beyond the safe harbor of prepress and manufacturing—publicity, marketing, sales, distribution, and fulfillment. Special thanks to Peter Dougherty, Jack Goellner, Joanna Hurley, Altie Karper, and Barbara Lamb. I am also grateful to William Bishop, Michael Donatelli, Calvin Luther Martin, Ted Parkhurst, Ken Sabol, and Tim Sullivan.

However, it was my in-house professional help that really made the book come alive. It was my husband Peter's unique talent in managing the production of complex, high-quality books on tight schedules that transformed this project from the potential to the real. More important, his love and partnering during the past seventeen years of our marriage transformed my very life from the potential to the real. The name Peter comes from the Greek word for *rock*. He is indeed my rock.

Those friends who saved the book from depending on my pictures alone deserve special thanks, beyond mere photo credits: Glenn Jenks, Doug Stavoe, Suzie Wilson, and Marge Jenkins.

Finally, my thanks to all those who in their own countless and unique ways aided me—often unknowingly—on the journey that led to the book you now hold in your hands: Hank and Loretta Bercuk, Jean and Charles Blevins, Jean Carey, Bob and Marty Christopher, John Clark, the Dunlop-Kearney family, Wayne Fulcher, Dick and Mary George, Nick and Sherron Hodgkinson, Mario Iacono, Terri Kasten, Mary Lopuch, Mikel McClain, Timothy Radden, the Sadick family (Osama, Joan, Susie, and Adam), Paulette and Walter Schiff, the Stavoe family, Cathy Sullivan, the Tysenn family (Tom, Gina, and Adri), Inge and Robert Vairo, the Good Shepherd of the Hills Education for Ministry program participants (1998–2003), the Education for Ministry mentor training groups (Santa Fe, September 2000; Tucson, September 2001; Los Angeles, January 2003), and the faith communities of Good Shepherd of the Hills Episcopal Church, Cave Creek, Arizona, and All Saints' Episcopal Church, Princeton, New Jersey.

NOTES

Prologue

1   "The first going-down into the desert . . . ," Van Dyke, p. 23. Van Dyke actually spent very little time in the desert and relied heavily on his imagination, as explained in Peter Wild's introduction. Even so, I found some of Van Dyke's descriptions to be succinct, colorful, and entertaining.

1   Although the Sonoran Desert is eight million years old, the current community of plants and animals seen in Arizona has been in place for only about four thousand years. During the last ice age, the Desert receded south of Tucson, but as the climate warmed it expanded northward.

2   Throughout the book, I use the capitalized form *Desert* to signify the persona of the desert—its unique and mysterious presence.

3   The voice of one calling in the desert echoes Isaiah 40:3. The voice of the desert is echoing the title of Krutch's book, which is an excellent account of the natural history and living community of the Sonoran Desert mixed with personal thoughts and experiences. Krutch wrote that the best use of a desert is contemplation (see p. 221).

Chapter One

5   "Consider frequently the connection of all things . . . ," Marcus Aurelius, p. 63 (VI.38). Throughout the notes, the number of the individual meditation is given in parentheses after the page number.

7   "It would be well, perhaps . . . ," Thoreau, p. 283.

8   "We praise You, Lord, for Sister Moon . . . ," http://www.prayerfoundation.org/canticle_of_brother_sun.htmon, accessed October 22, 2003. This poem was originally titled "The Canticle of the Creatures."

9   "The stars are the apexes . . . ," Thoreau, pp. 265–66.

10   "The light which puts out . . . ," Thoreau, p. 572.

10   For a helpful description of why we see a blue sky, see Phillips et al., p. 55.

11   "And not by eastern windows only . . .", http://www.theotherpages.org/poems/clough01.html#1, accessed October 25, 2003.

12   "Looking at these stars . . . ," Wells, p. 76.

12   "The universe is either a confusion . . . ," Marcus Aurelius, p. 56 (VI.10).

13   "Nature has no one distinguishable . . . ," James, p. 382. Although James wrote these words around 1900, they seem appropriate today amid scientists' questions about the purpose of the universe and such natural processes as evolution.

14   The concept of embracing otherness is prominent in the writings of the thirteenth-century

German mystic Meister Eckhart. Although Eckhart's writings are somewhat challenging to understand, he was a brilliant, unorthodox preacher and mystic, ahead of his time and ostracized by the church. He was highly regarded by twentieth-century Catholic theologian Thomas Merton.

14 "I hear you whispering there . . . ," Whitman, p. 71.

15 For more information on the life cycle of stars and the role of neutrinos in supernova explosions, see Cole and Smolin, Chapters 3 and 8.

17 "Our inventions are wont to be pretty toys . . . ," Thoreau, p. 306.

19 "Was somebody asking . . . ," Whitman, p. 18.

20 "As with our colleges . . . ," Thoreau, p. 306.

22 It is highly inaccurate to consider "the Hebrews" as a unified group with a common set of beliefs from Abraham to Jesus. The fact that there are often two or more versions of the same story (e.g., the Creation story in the early part of Genesis) attests to the disparate views among the Hebrews. Throughout this book, references to the Hebrews and their beliefs should be taken as highlighted aspects of their story, rather than a comprehensive historical account of who believed what when. For more information about the Hebrews' history and the origins of the Old Testament, see Meeks, especially pp. xvii–xxx and 3–5.

23 The Old Testament has had quite a history, compiled by many contributors over some eighteen centuries. Most of the Old Testament stories and history were passed down orally for many centuries. The sacred status given to its contents by the Hebrews was awarded in hindsight, not at the time the stories were first conceived. Apparently, very little of the Old Testament was written down until the Hebrew captivity in Babylon in the sixth century BC. Originally derived from the Phoenician alphabet, the Hebrew alphabet has no vowels. Thus it can be difficult to interpret, leaving the meaning of certain words, phrases, and passages to subjective interpretation to a greater extent than in other written languages. The final written version was not canonized (recognized as sacred) until about AD 100, partly as a reaction to the development of Christianity. Most Christian denominations recognize the official Hebrew version as the Old Testament, except that the Roman Catholic Church recognizes the Apocrypha as scripture.

23 The first chapter of Genesis includes some of the latest writing of the Old Testament. This is evident in the justification for the Sabbath in Genesis Chapter 1 (thought to have been added by priestly writers), which is missing from the earlier version of the Creation story contained in Genesis Chapter 2.

24 The term *word* means a symbol that communicates a thought. The word of God is an expansive concept, suggesting the comprehensive, organized thoughts of God that bring order to the cosmos and the human mind—conceptually similar to the unified theory that scientists seek to explain how the universe works.

29 The Pharisees, Sadducees, and scribes were the religious leaders during Jesus' lifetime. Both the Pharisees and the Sadducees were strict fundamentalists with regard to the law of Moses (the Torah). However, the Pharisees revered both the written and the oral forms of the Torah, while the Sadducees relied on only the writeen form. The scribes were religious scholars.

34 "All praise, my Lord, through Sister Earth . . . ," http://www.prayerfoundation.org/canticle_of_brother_sun.htmon, accessed October 22, 2003.

35 "Each is not for its own sake . . . ," Whitman, p. 15.

Chapter Two

37   "Earth! you seem to look . . . ," Whitman, p. 60.

40   "The dark thunder-clouds that occasionally . . . ," Van Dyke, p. 33.

41   "What is the pill which will keep . . . ," Thoreau, p. 389.

43   "It is a gaunt land . . . ," Van Dyke, p. 26.

44   "Forsaken of their kind . . . ," Van Dyke, p. 1.

48   "See revolving the globe . . . ," Whitman, pp. 11–12.

48   For a descriptive narrative on plate tectonics, see McPhee.

52   "The atmosphere is not a perfume . . . ," Whitman, p. 22.

53   "We praise you, Lord, for Brothers Wind and Air . . . ," http://www.prayerfoundation.org/canticle_of_brother_sun.htmon, accessed October 22, 2003.

55   For additional information on the Hebrews' idolatry, see note for p. 85.

63   "We praise and bless You, Lord, and give You thanks . . . ," http://www.prayerfoundation.org/canticle_of_brother_sun.htmon, accessed October 22, 2003.

64   "The press of my foot to the earth . . . ," Whitman, p. 32.

65   "No politics, song, religion, behavior . . . ," Whitman, p. 181.

66   *For this Earth . . . ,* inspired by the first stanza of "Annabel Lee" by Edgar Allan Poe.

Chapter Three

69   "God has made all things that are made . . . ," Julian of Norwich, p. 19.

70   For more information about the origins of the Sonoran Desert, see Phillips, especially pp. 51–61.

71   "None of the brute creation . . . ," Thoreau, pp. 267–69.

73   "There is no living in concord . . . ," Van Dyke, p. 27.

73   "There is, however, only one reptile . . . ," Van Dyke, p. 168.

75   "There is a war of elements . . . ," Van Dyke, p. 26.

77   "The spotted hawk swoops by . . . ," Whitman, p. 73.

78   "I have called this principle . . . ," http://www.bartleby.com/100/450.1.html, accessed July 22, 2003.

78   For a detailed account of the early evolution of life on earth, see Gould, especially Chapter 1.

80   "From the war of nature . . . ," http://www.bartleby.com/66/85.15785.html, accessed July 22, 2003.

80   This is a very brief account of life's fascinating evolutionary history over the past 500 million years. For an interesting perspective on how life evolved, see Lockley, particularly Chapter 2. For more in-depth information on the causes and effects of mass extinction events, see Leakey and Lewin, especially Chapters 2–5, and Gould, Chapter 3.

80   "I love to see that Nature . . . ," Thoreau, p. 557.

82   "And as to you Death, you bitter hug of mortality . . . ," Whitman, p. 71.

84   Regarding scientists' concerns about a sixth major extinction currently unfolding, see Leakey and Lewin, Chapter 13, and Wilson, pp. 98–101. Although extinctions normally occur in Nature, Leakey and Lewin indicate that the current extinction rate is 120,000 times normal (p. 241). It is not difficult to conclude that this is true when one considers that the global population had increased from about one billion in the year 1800 to over six billion by the year 2000. (Population statistics from http://www.prb.org/Content/

NavigationMenu/PRB/Educators/Human_Population/Population_Growth/Population_Growth.htm, accessed October 27, 2003.)

85   Jaynes suggests that the use of the plural form of the word for God (*elohim*) in parts of Genesis and the Hebrews' difficulties with idolatry were linked to the hallucinations common in human consciousness at that time, which were mistaken for the voices of the gods (see pp. 297–98).

94   "The love of life, at any and every level . . . ," James, p. 392.

95   "The answer came . . . ," Julian of Norwich, pp. 9–10.

95   "To cooperate in the highest . . . ," Thoreau, p. 326.

95   "Who goes there? Hankering, gross . . . ," Whitman, p. 37.

Chapter Four

99   "The prime characteristic of cosmic . . . ," Bucke, p. 3.

101   "There can be no very black melancholy . . . ," Thoreau, p. 382.

102   "One impulse from a vernal wood . . . ," http://www.age-of-the-sage.org/poets/william_wordsworth.html, accessed October 25, 2003.

105   "Man with all his noble qualities . . . ," http://www.bartleby.com66/85.15783.html, accessed July 22, 2003.

106   "Hurrah for positive science! . . . ," Whitman, p. 41.

107   "I think I could turn and live with animals . . . ," Whitman, p. 48.

108   For a detailed summary of human evolution, including maps of likely migration patterns, see Gould, Chapter 6. See Tattersall for a more up-to-date and concise account.

108   Krutch comments that the great mystery of evolution is not that changing conditions stimulated new adaptations, but why the ability to respond to the new demands in certain ways, but not others, was inherent in living organisms (see pp. 148–49). This is certainly true with human evolution. Why did some primates walk upright to look for food when others did not?

108   "Could a greater miracle take place . . . ," Thoreau, p. 266. Although Thoreau was referring to aliens in this passage, I believe it applies to humans as well, given how unknowable we are to one another at some level.

109   Arsuaga gives an insightful account of our Neanderthal relatives and their remarkable abilities and accomplishments.

109   Humor and artistic expressions are also unique to humans.

109   That sexual intimacy helped *Homo sapiens* to survive better is also suggested by the fact that it takes some effort to learn the timing of a given human female's ovulation, whereas for other species this task is relatively easy. This fact suggests that sexual intimacy serves a purpose beyond procreation for humans.

109   "What behaved well in the past . . . ," Whitman, p. 40.

110   "Every child begins the world again . . . ," Thoreau, p. 283.

110   A comprehensive overview of the brain's structure and the role played by the reptilian, mammalian, and human brains is provided in Carter, Chapter 1.

110   Given the integrated nature of the physical and psychic aspects of the human brain, it is difficult to overestimate the importance of proper nutrition, sleep, hydration, exercise, stress minimization, and relaxation for optimal physical and mental health. A balanced

diet is critical to the maintenance not only of important bodily functions such as immunity but also of consciousness. For example, essential fatty acids (found in eggs, fish, nuts, olives, seeds, and other foods) play a major role in maintaining brain chemistry and have been linked to enhanced health and longevity in such areas as the Mediterranean and the Japanese island of Okinawa. These acids have probably been readily available in the human diet for many thousands (if not millions) of years, so the unconscious mind and the body have no doubt come to depend on them more than sporadically available foods like meat.

111   "We are conscious of an animal in us . . . ," Thoreau, p. 465.

111   "I have always been regretting . . . ," Thoreau, p. 351.

112   For a detailed account of the functions of the left and right hemispheres of the cortex and the role of the corpus callosum in sharing information between them, see Carter, Chapter 2.

112   If women have better wiring for consciousness, it is curious that civilization has had such a distinct inclination toward patriarchy (as opposed to the more egalitarian hunter-gatherer lifestyle). Jaynes observes that a marked increase in sexuality and the use of phallic symbols appeared in the art of Greece in the seventh century BC. The physical appearance of the male erection clearly had a potent effect on the newly conscious mind and on sexual fantasies (see pp. 465–67). Probably as a result, maleness became associated with observable power.

112   "As I see my soul reflected in Nature . . . ," Whitman, p. 79.

114   A helpful discussion of the difference between mammalian emotions from the limbic system and conscious feelings from the cortex is provided in Carter, Chapter 4.

115   "The incessant strain and anxiety of some . . . ," Thoreau, p. 266.

115   Jung claimed that the modern human consciousness, even in highly civilized countries, was unstable and susceptible to fragmentation. For an interesting discussion of the relationship problems of the unconscious and conscious minds in the modern Western psyche, see Jung (1964), pp. 72–94.

115   For additional information on the collective unconscious, see Jung (1933), pp. 71–73.

116   "I rejoice that there are owls . . . ," Thoreau, p. 377.

117   Bucke provides an interesting perspective on the evolution of human consciousness, including evidence of advanced states of consciousness in Buddha, Moses, Isaiah, Lao-tse, Jesus, Paul, Mohammed, Whitman, Thoreau, and many others.

129   "Along with the consciousness . . . ," Bucke, p. 3.

130   "It is hard to have a Southern overseer . . . ," Thoreau, p. 263.

131   "And I have by me, for my comfort . . . ," Wells, p. 115.

Chapter Five

133   "The highest possible stage in moral culture . . . ," http://www.bartleby.com/66/81.15781 .html, accessed July 22, 2003.

136   "What finally became of them . . . ," Van Dyke, p. 20.

140   "Most of the luxuries . . . ," Thoreau, pp. 269–70.

141   "The mind of the universe is social," Marcus Aurelius, p. 53 (V.30).

142   "The friendly and flowing savage . . . ," Whitman, p. 59.

143   "I see the constructiveness of my race . . . ," Whitman, p. 116.

143   Jaynes makes a compelling case that consciousness is accessed through language, and that

modern self-consciousness slowly developed concurrently with spoken and written modern languages (see Chapter 6). The form of self-consciousness that we experience today began to appear around 1200 BC in Mesopotamia (see pp. 453–54). For example, the first written indication of a sense of guilt appeared in the literary works of Homer in ancient Greece some 2,800 years ago (see pp. 257–72). However, as this new form of consciousness developed, the human mind began to be subject to hallucinations similar to those that a schizophrenic experiences. These imagined voices were thought to be the voices of the gods. The first archaeological evidence of a god dates to about 9000 BC, supporting this theory (see pp. 138–45).

144   "'All the same,' said the Scarecrow . . . ," Baum, p. 28.

145   "While civilization has been improving . . . ," Thoreau, p. 289.

145   "A spider is proud when it has caught a fly . . . ," Marcus Aurelius, p. 107 (X.10).

145   For an informative and fascinating description of the archaeological evidence of war, see Ferguson.

146   "Do you not see the little plants . . . ," Marcus Aurelius, p. 44 (V.1).

147   "Most men, even in this comparatively . . . ," Thoreau, p. 261.

148   "This conjunction of an immense . . . ," Eisenhower's farewell address from http://www.eisenhower.utexas.edu/farewell.htm, accessed October 25, 2003.

149   "I cannot believe that our factory system . . . ," Thoreau, p. 281.

163   "I believe that men are generally still . . . ," Thoreau, p. 382.

164   *Waiting for Godot* is the title of a 1952 play by the Irish author Samuel Beckett, which relates the self-inflicted hopelessness of two characters who continue to wait for someone they know will never come.

165   "They shall arise in the States . . . ," Whitman, p. 381.

Chapter Six

167   "I know of no more encouraging fact . . . ," Thoreau, p. 343.

169   "Life is more like wrestling . . . ," Marcus Aurelius, p. 76 (VII.61).

173   "I say, beware of all enterprises . . . ," Thoreau, p. 278.

173   For more on the definition of a paradigm, see Kuhn, p. 23. On how crisis indicates an opportunity for retooling, see p. 76. On rejecting one paradigm before another has been accepted, see p. 79. For a discussion of how science is portrayed in textbooks, see p. 140.

174   "The unexamined life is not . . . ," http://www.quotationspage.com, accessed October 25, 2003. Attributed by Plato to Socrates, "Apology."

176   "Our moulting season . . . ," Thoreau, p. 279.

177   "Repentance is a kind of self-reproof . . . ," Marcus Aurelius, p. 81 (VIII.10).

177   "Why did I walk through crowds . . . ," Dickens, p. 32. Although these words appear in the book after the following quote, they summarize his remorse the best.

177   "Business! Mankind was my business . . . ," Dickens, pp. 31–32.

178   "You fear the world too much . . . ," Dickens, p. 55.

178   "Will you decide what men shall live . . . ," Dickens, p. 79.

179   "The best repentance is to up and act . . . ," James, p. 114.

183   The teachings of Zoroaster are the basis for the Persian religion Zoroastrianism, which had a profound influence on both Judaism and Christianity. In Asia, Taoism, Confucianism, and Buddhism were based on the teachings of Lao-tse, Confucius, and

Buddha, respectively. These Asian religions shared a foundation in nonviolence, which was to be a prominent theme of Jesus' teachings several centuries later.

188   The four gospels were written in Greek several decades after Jesus' death by different authors, and for different audiences. The Gospel of Mark was probably written first, in the late AD 60s, possibly by an eyewitness to Jesus' ministry who was then living beyond Palestine. Written with an especially harsh attitude toward the Pharisees, the Gospel of Matthew was probably written in AD 80–90, and was most likely attributed to the apostle Matthew in order to gain credibility. With a notable emphasis on compassion, the Gospel of Luke was written around the same time as that of Matthew; its account gives particular prominence to the role of women in Jesus' life and ministry. Because Matthew and Luke appear to be based in part on Mark, they are referred to as the synoptic gospels. The last to be written, the Gospel of John, has little in common with the other gospels and places a greater emphasis on the mystical dimensions of Jesus' life and teachings. It was possibly written by a member of a group of Christians expelled from a synagogue in the AD 90s, so its references to "the Jews" were probably not meant to signify the Jewish people so much as the local Jewish community.

196   "Throw away vain hopes . . . ," Marcus Aurelius, p. 32 (V.14).

196   The estimate of 44 million uninsured people is from the U.S. Census Bureau, http://story .news.yahoo.com/news?tmpl=story2&cid=1506&u=/afp/us_health_insurance&ncid=, accessed October 26, 2003.

196   The estimate of 10 million or more illegal immigrants is based on information from the Center for Immigration Studies, http://www.cis.org/topics/currentnumbers.html, accessed October 21, 2003.

196   The estimate of 9 million unemployed people is from the Department of Labor, http://data.bls.gov/cgi-bin/surveymost, accessed October 21, 2003. It is worth noting that many more millions of underemployed Americans are not included in this estimate.

196   The estimate of 4 million homeless people is from the National Coalition for the Homeless, http://www.nationalhomeless.org/numbers.html, accessed October 21, 2003.

197   See Doyle for estimates of billionaires in the world and in the United States.

197   "And I saw quite clearly how much God . . . ," Julian of Norwich, p. 10. Julian suggests that the soul's yearnings for God are caused by the Holy Spirit.

Chapter Seven

199   "We and God have business with each other . . . ," James, p. 399.

200   "I seize the descending man . . . ," Whitman, p. 60.

203   "I believe that in every little thing . . . ," Teresa of Avila, p. 81.

203   "The mass of men lead lives of quiet desperation . . . ," Thoreau, p. 263.

205   "O happy living things! no tongue . . . ," Bryant, p. 648. The quote appears at the end of Part IV of the poem.

206   "It is a shame when the soul is first . . . ," Marcus Aurelius, p. 61 (VI.29).

208   "Since the sense of Presence of a higher and friendly power . . . ," James, p. 222.

208   "Religion . . . shall mean for us . . . ," James, p. 42.

208   "I believe in you my soul . . . ," Whitman, p. 25.

209   "The uneasiness, reduced to its simplest terms . . . ," James, p. 393.

209   "He becomes conscious that this higher part . . . ," James, pp. 393–94.

209	"If religion is to mean anything definite for us . . . ," James, p. 55.
210	"At these places at least, I say . . . ," James, p. 406.
210	"It does not follow, because our ancestors . . . ," James, p. 388.
210	For more information about the role of faith, see James, pp. 391–92.
211	"Let me then propose, as an hypothesis . . . ," James, p. 396.
211	"Does God really exist? How does he exist . . . ," James, pp. 392, 400.
211	"All parts of the universe are interwoven . . . ," Marcus Aurelius, p. 69 (VII.9).
211	Statistics regarding the percentage of the world's population adhering to various religions are from http://www.adherents.com/Religions_By_Adherents.html, accessed February 23, 2003.
213	For more information about the connection between the world's major religions and the desert, visit www.desertspirituality.com.
213	"Gods' Own Country," see Maugham, p. 312.
215	"The conservation of natural resources . . . ," http://theodoreroosevelt.org/life/conservation.html, accessed September 4, 2003.
215	Twelve-step programs have made a significant contribution to civilization in aiding recovery from various types of addiction. For more information about the twelve steps, the universal spiritual values underlying Alcoholics Anonymous, and the growth of Alcoholics Anonymous into a worldwide organization, visit www.aa.org.
223	Regarding Jesus' reformation of Judaism as a religion of the conscious, see Jaynes, p. 318.
228	"The universe . . . takes a turn genuinely for the worse . . . ," James, pp. 399–400.
228	"We praise You, Lord, for all . . . ," http://www.prayerfoundation.org/canticle_of_brother_sun.htm, accessed October 22, 2003.
229	*For this Creator lives . . . ,* inspired by the first stanza of "Annabel Lee" by Edgar Allan Poe.
229	Marcus Aurelius remarked on how earthly things reflect the orderly combination of contraries (attributed to Plato; see Meditation VII.48). Teilhard de Chardin found that the essential marvel of the divine presence was its ability to harmonize qualities that appear to us to be contradictory (1968, p. 113).
230	The word *harmony* is derived from the Greek word for joint; it is defined as the pleasing interaction or appropriate combination of the elements in a whole.
230	"In eternity there is indeed something . . . ," Thoreau, p. 349.

BIBLIOGRAPHY AND
SUGGESTED READINGS

We are today constantly confronted with insights into spirituality claiming to be new. It is difficult to know which are truly original without an understanding of Western spiritual traditions. This reading list includes material quoted and otherwise referred to in the text and notes, as well as other works that can be especially helpful in learning more about the physical and spiritual underpinnings of our world.

The spiritual essence of the Old and New Testaments is most easily accessed through the following three books of the Bible: the Book of Psalms, the Gospel of Mark, and the Book of James (NIV versions).

Alvarez, Walter. *T. rex and the Crater of Doom*. Princeton, N.J.: Princeton University Press, 1997.

Arsuaga, Juan Luis. "Requiem for a Heavyweight," *Natural History*, December 2002/January 2003, pp. 43–48.

Baum, L. Frank. *The Wizard of Oz*. New York: Penguin, 1998 (1900).

Bryant, William Cullen, editor. *The Library of World Poetry*. New York: Avenel, n.d.

Bucke, Richard Maurice. *Cosmic Consciousness*. New York: Penguin, 1991 (1901).

Carter, Rita. *Mapping the Mind*. Berkeley: University of California Press, 1999.

Chronic, Halka. *Roadside Geology of Arizona*. Missoula, Mont.: Mountain Press, 1998 (1983).

Cole, K. C. "Fun with Physics," *The New Yorker*, June 2, 2003, pp. 48–57.

Dickens, Charles. *A Christmas Carol*. New York: Airmont, 1963 (1844).

Doorn, Peter L., and Troy L. Péwé. *Geologic and Gravimetric Investigations of the Carefree Basin, Maricopa County, Arizona*. Tucson: Arizona Geological Society, 1991.

Doyle, Rodger. "The Rich and Other Americans," *Scientific American*, February 2001, p. 26.

Einstein, Albert. *The Expanded Quotable Einstein*, edited by Alice Calaprice. Princeton, N.J.: Princeton University Press, 2000.

Ferguson, R. Brian. "The Birth of War," *Natural History*, July/August 2003, pp. 28–35.

Fischer, Louis. *Gandhi: His Life and Message for the World*. New York: Penguin, 1954.

Francis of Assisi. *The Canticle of Brother Sun*.

Frankl, Viktor E. *Man's Search for Meaning*. New York: Simon and Schuster, 1984 (1959).

Gould, Stephen Jay. *The Book of Life*. New York: W. W. Norton, 2001 (1993).

Grun, Bernard. *The Timetables of History*. New York: Simon and Schuster, 1982 (1946).

Hammarskjöld, Dag. *Markings*. New York: Ballantine, 1993 (1964).

Huxley, Aldous. *The Perennial Philosophy*. New York: Harper and Row, 1970 (1944).

James, William. *The Varieties of Religious Experience*. New York: Simon and Schuster, 1997 (1902).

Jaynes, Julian. *The Origin of Consciousness in the Breakdown of the Bicameral Mind.* New York: Houghton Mifflin, 1990.

Julian of Norwich. *Revelation of Love,* translated by John Skinner. New York: Doubleday, 1997.

Jung, Carl G. *Modern Man in Search of a Soul.* New York: Harcourt, 1933.

———. *Man and His Symbols.* New York: Dell, 1964.

Krutch, Joseph Wood. *The Voice of the Desert: A Naturalist's Interpretation.* New York: William Sloane, 1971 (1954).

Kuhn, Thomas S. *The Structure of Scientific Revolutions.* 3rd ed. Chicago: University of Chicago Press, 1996 (1962).

Leakey, Richard, and Roger Lewin. *The Sixth Extinction: Patterns of Life and the Future of Humankind.* New York: Anchor/Doubleday, 1995.

Leopold, Aldo. *A Sand County Almanac.* New York: Ballantine, 1970 (1949).

Lewis, C. S. *The Abolition of Man.* San Francisco: HarperSanFrancisco, 1974 (1944).

Lockley, Martin. *The Eternal Trail: A Tracker Looks at Evolution.* Reading, Mass.: Perseus, 1999.

Marcus Aurelius. *Meditations.* Roslyn, N.Y.: Walter Black, 1945.

Maugham, W. Somerset. *The Razor's Edge.* New York: Penguin Books, 1992 (1944).

McPhee, John. *Basin and Range.* New York: Noonday Press/Farrar, Straus and Giroux, 1990 (1981).

Meeks, Wayne A., general editor. *The HarperCollins Study Bible, New Revised Standard Version.* New York: HarperCollins, 1993.

Meister Eckhart. *The Essential Sermons, Commentaries, Treatises, and Defense,* translated by Edmund College and Bernard McGinn. Mahwah, N.J.: Paulist Press, 1981.

Merton, Thomas. *The Seven Storey Mountain.* New York: Harcourt Brace, 1948.

Phillips, Steven J., and Patricia Wentworth Comus, editors. *A Natural History of the Sonoran Desert.* Tucson: Arizona-Sonora Desert Museum Press, 2000.

Smolin, Lee. *The Life of the Cosmos.* New York: Oxford University Press, 1997.

Tattersall, Ian. "How We Came to Be," *Scientific American,* February 2001, pp. 56–63.

Teilhard de Chardin, Pierre. *The Phenomenon of Man.* New York: Harper and Row, 1975 (1959).

———. *The Divine Milieu.* New York: Harper and Row, 1968 (1960).

———. *Christianity and Evolution.* New York: Harcourt Brace, 1971.

Teresa of Avila. *Interior Castle,* edited and translated by E. Allison Peers. New York: Doubleday, 1989 (1961).

Thoreau, Henry David. *Walden,* in *The Portable Thoreau,* edited by Carl Bode. New York: Penguin, 1982 (1854).

Van Dyke, John C. *The Desert: Further Studies in Natural Appearances.* Baltimore: The Johns Hopkins University Press, 1999 (1901).

Wells, H. G. *The Time Machine.* New York: Bantam, 1991 (1895).

Whitman, Walt. *Leaves of Grass.* New York: Bantam, 1983 (1892).

Wiesel, Elie. *Night.* New York: Bantam, 1982 (1960).

Wilson, Edward O. *The Future of Life.* New York: Alfred A. Knopf, 2002.

✺ INDEX ✺

The page on which a concept is first defined or explained is set in italics. Page numbers followed by f refer to figures.

Hebrews: Abraham's covenant with God, 55, 56, 152, 219, 221; Babylonian exile of, 183; communities of, 150–51; enslavement in Egypt, 56; Exodus of, 56, 152–53; holistic view of humans, 181; idols (baals) worshiped by, 55–56, 58, 85, 183; kingdoms of, 25, 60, 182, 183, 186; kings of, 25; law of, 152, 155; monotheism of, 56, 58; priests of, 125, 154–56; Promised Land of, 55, 56–60, 85, 154, 221; prophets of, 182–87; relationship with God, 22–23, 24–25, 60, 87, 117–18, 123, 156, 181–82; relationship with Nature, 55, 84–89; religious leaders of, 28–29, 60, 61–63, 157, 223; Ten Commandments and, 58, 59–60; understanding of human nature, 117; views of women, 122

Hinduism, 211
Hohokam, 137–38, 140
Holocaust, 18
holy seed. See remnant
Holy Spirit, 161
homelessness, 196
Homer, 144
hominids, 106, 108, 142
Homo habilis, 108
Homo sapiens, 110
honeybees, 206
Hosea, 183
human brain, 110; capacity, 108; components of, 110, 111; cortex, 110, 111–12, 143, 144; evolution of, 117; frontal lobe, 112, 114, 143, 160; "left" and "right," 112; mammalian brain, 110, 111; occipital lobe, 112, 160; parietal lobe, 112, 160; purpose of, 117; reptilian brain, 110, 111; temporal lobe, 112, 143, 160
human genome. See genes
humans: communities of, 142; differences from other animals, 108; evolution of, 105–6, 108–10; genetic influences on, 106–8; similarities to other animals, 105, 110
humility, 63–65

hummingbirds, 100–105
hydrogen. See dark energy

idols, 55–56, 58, 85, 183, 191
illegal immigrants, 196
Incas, 143
inner child, 115
inner mammal. See mammals
inner reptile. See reptiles
insects, 81, 172, 206. See also arthropods
Iraq, 20
Isaac, 222
Isaiah, 34, 183, 184–87
Islam, 211
Israel, kingdom of, 25, 182, 183, 186

James, William, 208–11
javelinas, 134
Jeremiah, 183
Jesus: birth of, 60, 156; on community, 157, 159–60, 161; death of, 226–27; in Desert, 33, 188–91; on devil, 90–93; disciples of, 159; on evil, 89; on faith, 223–24; healing by, 62, 223–24; Hebrew religious leaders and, 28–29, 62, 223; humility of, 63; identity of, 124; influence of David on, 26; interaction with Earth, 61–63, 65; Isaiah and, 187; on kingdom of God, 30–33, 34, 65, 126–28, 129; level of consciousness of, 128, 160; life of, 28, 60–61, 188; ministry of, 33–34, 61, 125, 188, 192; miracles of, 62–63; mission of, 223; on new covenant, 157–59, 161; nonviolence advocated by, 224–27; parables told by, 28, 29–30, 90, 161, 193–94; prayers of, 126; on righteousness, 28–29; seed and plant metaphors of, 90, 93; as son of man, 128; on spiritual freedom, 93–94; temptations by Satan, 190–91; view of God, 124–25, 126; view of human spirituality, 30
John the Baptist, 188, 193
Joshua, 59
Judah, kingdom of, 25, 183, 186
Judaism, 211, 223. See also Hebrews

Judean Desert, 188
Julian of Norwich, Lady, 94–95
Jung, Carl Gustav, 115
justice, 126, 218

Kennedy, John F., 216
King, Martin Luther, Jr., 224
kingdom of God, 30–33, 34, 65, 126–28, 129
kingdom of heaven. See kingdom of God
Korea, 18
Kuhn, Thomas, 173, 174

land of the free, 147–48
languages: development of writing, 144; Greek, 156, 192; modern, 143; stimulation of consciousness by, 143, 144
Lao-tse, 183
law, 152, 155. See also Ten Commandments
left brain, 112
life on Earth, 76, 78–79, 80–81, 94, 95. See also evolution
light, speed of, 13
lightning, 53
Little Dipper, 9, 10, 229
living God, 163
lizards, 71–73, 204
Lone Mountain, 9
love, 109, 125

Malachai, 183
mammals: brains of, 110, 111; emotions of, 114; evolution of, 81, 82; javelinas, 134; marine, 141; primates, 106, 141
mass extinctions. See extinctions
matter, 14
Maugham, W. Somerset, 213
Mayas, 143
Meister Eckhart, 94
mercy, 125–26
metanoia, 174–76; effects of, 179–81, 186, 193; Jesus' experience of, 190; portrayed in movies, 176–79; righteousness and, 196; translations of Greek word, 192